PUNISHING THE DARKNESS

HARRISON HOUSE BOOKS BY JOSEPH Z

Punishing the Darkness: Spiritual Warfare That Works

Punishing the Darkness Study Manual

Demystifying the Prophetic: Understanding the Voice of God for the Coming Days of Fire

Demystifying the Prophetic Study Manual

The Secret to the Life of John: A Revelation for a Supernaturally Long-Lasting Life

Servants of Fire: Secrets of the Unseen War & Angels Fighting for You

Breaking Hell's Economy: Your Guide to Last-Days Supernatural Provision

Breaking Hell's Economy Study Manual

The Spirit of Elijah: Expose the Truth. Embrace God's Power. Break the Antichrist Spirit.

The Spirit of Elijah Study Manual

A Prophet's Reward: Partnering with the Prophetic for Your Faith, Favor, and Financial Miracles

Weaponizing Your Faith: Supernaturally Equipped to Receive Your Breakthrough

The Origin of the Cosmic Battle

Jesus and the Kingmakers

- STUDY MANUAL -

PUNISHING THE DARKNESS

SPIRITUAL WARFARE THAT WORKS

JOSEPH Z

Published by Harrison House Publishers
Shippensburg, PA 17257

ISBN 13 TP: 9781667512457
ISBN 13 eBook: 9781667512464

For Worldwide Distribution, Printed in the U.S.A.
1 2 3 4 5 6 7 8 / 30 29 28 27 26

CONTENTS

LETTER FROM JOSEPH

Dear Reader,

As you navigate through your life, it is essential to remember that you possess God-given power and authority designed to overcome the forces of spiritual darkness that seek to influence our world.

In First John 5:4, we are reminded that "whatever is born of God overcomes the world." This assurance speaks to the power of your faith—an incredible force that can bring the world and its values to their knees. As you read and work through the *Punishing the Darkness* book and study manual, may you recognize that your faith is a conquering power, a means through which you can actively engage with and challenge the cultural narratives around you.

This journey is not just about individual triumph but about collectively confronting the larger forces that seek to shape our society. It's crucial to understand that spiritual darkness uses humanity to advance its agenda. Therefore, those who control the culture significantly shape the narrative of our generation. With this understanding, my aim in this book, *Punishing the Darkness Study Manual*, is to equip you with the knowledge and tools needed to address the pressing issues we face today and to take you on a journey of discovery as you engage in times of self-focus and personal reflection points.

Within these pages, you will find a wealth of scriptural insights and references, along with the tools needed to navigate and confront the cultural challenges that are prevalent in our time. You will also encounter thought-provoking questions that will encourage you to dive deeper until you reach true revelation. From artificial intelligence to climate change and beyond, it is vital to engage with these issues from a standpoint of faith and authority. Remember, as believers in Christ, we are part of the *Ekklesia*—the Church that stands firm against the gates of hell.

Be assured that *greater is He who is in you than he that is in the world* (*see* 1 John 4:4). You have been entrusted with the authority to impact your surroundings and influence the culture in a positive and victorious way.

As you work through this book, I encourage you to maintain an open heart, ready to receive new insights and take action in the face of adversity. Together, let us rise, expand our faith, and fulfill our divine purpose to *punish the darkness*.

For Jesus,
Joseph Z

Manual Instructions

The *Punishing the Darkness Study Manual* was created to help individuals deepen their understanding while reading *Punishing the Darkness*. This Manual is a companion to reading the book, with each section featuring questions and additional information for reflection. The answers are in the section you read in the book, but there's room for your thoughts and answers. The "focus points" and "personal reflections" are opportunities for you to delve deeper and seek the Lord for answers, fostering personal growth. Some questions may require your honesty; in moments of uncertainty, let the Holy Spirit guide you. May God bless you on your journey through *Punishing the Darkness: Spiritual Warfare That Works* and this accompanying Study Manual.

SECTION ONE

CONFRONTING THE SPIRIT OF THE AGE

CHAPTER ONE

PUNISHING DARK POWERS

SCRIPTURES

1. **Second Kings 6:17**—And Elisha prayed, and said, "Lord, I pray, open his eyes that he may see." Then the Lord opened the eyes of the young man, and he saw. And behold, the mountain was full of horses and chariots of fire all around Elisha.

2. **Second Kings 6:14-16**—Therefore he sent horses and chariots and a great army there, and they came by night and surrounded the city. [15] And when the servant of the man of God arose early and went out, there was an army, surrounding the city with horses and chariots. And his servant said to him, "Alas, my master! What shall we do?" [16] So he answered, "Do not fear, for those who are with us are more than those who are with them."

3. **Second Kings 6:18**—So when the Syrians came down to him, Elisha prayed to the Lord, and said, "Strike this people, I pray, with blindness." And He struck them with blindness according to the word of Elisha.

4. **Second Kings 6:19**—Now Elisha said to them, "This is not the way, nor is this the city. Follow me, and I will bring you to the man whom you seek." But he led them to Samaria.

5. **Psalm 2:4**—He who sits in the heavens shall laugh; the Lord shall hold them in derision.

6. **Second Kings 6:20-21**—So it was, when they had come to Samaria, that Elisha said, "Lord, open the eyes of these men, that they may see." And the Lord opened

their eyes, and they saw; and there they were, inside Samaria! [21] Now when the king of Israel saw them, he said to Elisha, "My father, shall I kill them? Shall I kill them?"

7. **Second Kings 6:22-23**—But he answered, "You shall not kill them. Would you kill those whom you have taken captive with your sword and your bow? Set food and water before them, that they may eat and drink and go to their master." [23] Then he prepared a great feast for them; and after they ate and drank, he sent them away and they went to their master. So the bands of Syrian raiders came no more into the land of Israel.

8. **Ephesians 3:20**—Now to Him who is able to do exceedingly abundantly above all that we ask or think, according to the power that works in us.

9. **First John 4:4**—You are of God, little children, and have overcome them, because He who is in you is greater than he who is in the world.

10. **Psalm 149:5-9**—Let the saints be joyful in glory; let them sing aloud on their beds. [6] Let the high praises of God be in their mouth, and a two-edged sword in their hand, [7] to execute vengeance on the nations, and punishments on the peoples; [8] to bind their kings with chains, and their nobles with fetters of iron; [9] to execute on them the written judgment—this honor have all His saints. Praise the Lord!

11. **Colossians 2:15**—Having disarmed principalities and powers, He made a public spectacle of them, triumphing over them in it.

12. **Psalm 34:7 KJV**—The angel of the Lord encampeth round about them that fear him, and delivereth them.

13. **Psalm 91:11 KJV**—For he shall give his angels charge over thee, to keep thee in all thy ways.

14. **Zechariah 9:8 KJV**—And I will encamp about mine house because of the army, because of him that passeth by, and because of him that returneth: and no oppressor shall pass through them any more: for now have I seen with mine eyes.

15. **Isaiah 63:9 KJV**—In all their affliction he was afflicted, and the angel of his presence saved them: in his love and in his pity he redeemed them; and he bare them and carried them all the days of old.

> 16. **Second Corinthians 10:5-6**—Casting down arguments and every high thing that exalts itself against the knowledge of God, bringing every thought into captivity to the obedience of Christ, [6] and being ready to ***punish all disobedience*** when your obedience is fulfilled.

Just as the King of Syria recognized Elisha as a threat, the devil is aware of those who threaten his plans. He attempts to instill fear, intimidation, and ultimately, destruction. Have you ever faced this kind of attack? If so, please explain your experience and how you overcame it.

____

____

____

____

____

____

____

____

____

____

THE SERVANT'S VANTAGE POINT

Elisha responded to his servant's question, saying, "Do not fear, for those who are with us are more than those who are with them." It's possible that Elisha could see the horses and the chariots of fire. There is significance in having someone spiritually mature to speak truth and encouragement in times of battle. Is there someone in your life who has helped you during difficult times? If so, please expound on your answer.

____

____

____

____

____

How can you be like Elisha and help others see the truth of the situation when fear has taken hold of them?

A MAN WITH GOD OUTNUMBERS AN ARMY WITHOUT GOD

Through Elisha's prayer, God struck the entire Syrian army with blindness and led them through the wilderness. Read 1 Corinthians 1:27. In what way does this scripture resonate with what took place with Elisha and the Syrian army?

TEN MILES LEADING A BLIND ARMY

God is always gracious and merciful. The devil has used countless people to do his bidding. Elisha allowed the Syrian army to leave unharmed and with full stomachs. Romans 2:4 NIV says, "Or do you show contempt for the riches of his kindness, forbearance and patience, not realizing that God's kindness is intended to lead you to repentance?" God desires the lost to be saved, which is why He is rich in kindness. Thank God we are not saved through condemnation and shame but through Jesus and God's kindness!

GOD WILL SURROUND YOUR ENEMIES

FOCUS POINT

A great army surrounded Elisha and those with him. In the natural, this brought fear to the servant and possibly those with Elisha. Knowing what we need, God wants us to ask Him for what we need or desire. The end of James 4:2 says, "Yet you do not have because you do not ask." Elisha asked God for two things: to open his servant's eyes to see the angelic army and that God would blind the Syrian military. These were big asks, yet God responded and gave Elisha what he asked for.

Are there things you have not brought to the Lord? Maybe you feel you don't deserve them, or it might seem like an impossible situation. Take this time to seek the Lord. Let Him search your heart and reveal why you have difficulty asking Him for things. If this does not relate to you, take this time to present yourself before the Lord and let His presence minister to you. Whichever of these thoughts pertain to you, please write your prayer and what you hear Him saying.

GOD IS GREATER!

God has given us everything we need to overcome every situation the enemy throws our way. Because of Jesus, we can defeat the spirit of Antichrist and be victorious. The revelation of this is vital. If you think you are defeated, you will be. If you believe and stand on the Word of God and Jesus, you will undoubtedly know that you have already won!

EXECUTING VENGEANCE ON THE DARKNESS

Looking at the two acts of war from Psalm 149:5-9, how have you applied these two things to your life? What can you do to make these two acts your go-to response at war?

ELISHA DID MORE THAN SEND THE ENEMIES AWAY, HE SHOWED THEM COMPLETE DEFEAT

The Syrian army surrounded the city and Elisha; however, after an encounter with the man of God, they were surrounded by their enemies. After reading through the scriptures listed in this section, in what ways do they bring peace and encourage you to defeat any enemy?

TIME TO TORMENT YOUR SPIRITUAL TORMENTORS

PERSONAL REFLECTIONS

God desires us to win every battle and become tormentors to the kingdom of darkness. Punishing the darkness starts with punishing disobedience. If a person walks in disobedience to the Lord and His Word, the by-product is that tormentors will have the upper hand. However, when disobedience is dealt with and a person stands in their God-given authority and revelation, every tormentor must bow to the King of kings and leave with their tail between their legs.

Take this time to reflect on yourself. Has disobedience hindered you from walking in your authority? Do you feel the enemy is winning in a specific area of your life? Ask the Lord to reveal what needs to be uprooted from your life, what caused the disobedience, and the steps you need to take to receive your breakthrough. Write down a prayer of repentance and what He shows you.

CHAPTER TWO

THE SECOND DARK TOWER

SCRIPTURES

1. **Revelation 9:1-2 NIV**—The fifth angel sounded his trumpet, and I saw a star that had fallen from the sky to the earth. The star was given the key to the shaft of the Abyss. [2] ***When he opened the Abyss, smoke rose from it like the smoke from a gigantic furnace.*** The sun and sky were darkened by the smoke from the Abyss.

2. **Genesis 11:1-6**—Now the whole earth had one language and one speech. [2] And it came to pass, as they journeyed from the east, that they found a plain in the land of Shinar, and they dwelt there. [3] Then they said to one another, "Come, let us make bricks and bake them thoroughly." They had brick for stone, and they had asphalt for mortar. [4] And they said, "Come, let us build ourselves a city, and a tower whose top is in the heavens; let us make a name for ourselves, lest we be scattered abroad over the face of the whole earth." [5] But the Lord came down to see the city and the tower which the sons of men had built. [6] And the Lord said, "Indeed the people are one and they all have one language, and this is what they begin to do; now nothing that they propose to do will be withheld from them."

3. **Genesis 10:8-10**—Cush begot Nimrod; he began to be a mighty one on the earth. [9] He was a mighty hunter before the Lord; therefore it is said, "Like Nimrod the mighty hunter before the Lord." [10] And the beginning of his kingdom was Babel, Erech, Accad, and Calneh, in the land of Shinar.

4. **Isaiah 14:14 KJV**—I will ascend above the heights of the clouds; I will be like the most High.

5. **Genesis 6:4**—There were giants on the earth in those days, and also afterward, when the sons of God came in to the daughters of men and they bore children to them. Those were the mighty men who were of old, men of renown.

6. **First Corinthians 15:45**—And so it is written, "The first man Adam became a living being." The last Adam became a life-giving spirit.

7. **Romans 10:7**—or, "Who will descend into the ***abyss***?" (that is, to bring Christ up from the dead).

8. **Luke 8:31**—And they begged Him that He would not command them to go out into the **abyss**.

9. **Revelation 9:1-2**—Then the fifth angel sounded: And I saw a star fallen from heaven to the earth. To him was given the key to the ***bottomless pit.*** [2] And he opened the **bottomless pit**, and smoke arose out of the pit like the smoke of a great furnace. So the sun and the air were darkened because of the smoke of the pit.

10. **Revelation 11:7**—When they finish their testimony, the beast that ascends out of the **bottomless pit** will make war against them, overcome them, and kill them.

11. **Revelation 17:8**—The beast that you saw was, and is not, and will ascend out of the **bottomless pit** and go to perdition. And those who dwell on the earth will marvel, whose names are not written in the Book of Life from the foundation of the world, when they see the beast that was, and is not, and yet is.

12. **Revelation 20:1-3**—Then I saw an angel coming down from heaven, having the key to the ***bottomless pit*** and a great chain in his hand. [2] He laid hold of the dragon, that serpent of old, who is the Devil and Satan, and bound him for a thousand years; [3] and he cast him into the ***bottomless pit,*** and shut him up, and set a seal on him, so that he should deceive the nations no more till the thousand years were finished. But after these things he must be released for a little while.

13. **Revelation 20:10**—The devil, who deceived them, was cast into the ***lake of fire*** and brimstone where the beast and the false prophet are. And they will be tormented day and night forever and ever.

14. **Revelation 9:11**—And they had as king over them the angel of the bottomless pit, whose name in Hebrew is Abaddon, but in Greek he has the name Apollyon.

15. **Matthew 16:18**—And I also say to you that you are Peter, and on this rock I will build My church, and the gates of Hades shall not prevail against it.

16. **Hebrews 10:38**—Now the just shall live by faith; but if anyone draws back, My soul has no pleasure in him.

17. **Galatians 1:4**—Who gave Himself for our sins, that He might deliver us from this present evil age, according to the will of our God and Father.

The devil has hated humanity from the very beginning. He despised God for putting man above him. Because of this, it has been his goal and desire to defeat the human race and send them all to hell. Sadly, many are succumbing to the dark deeds of the enemy and allowing him full access and control. As the *Ekklesia*, we are here to hold back the devil. Thank God for His Church!

SPIRITUAL FORCES OPERATE BY PERMISSION FOR ACCESS

Knowing that many are giving the devil full rein in their lives, how do you think the body of Christ should respond in this time? In what ways are you allowing God to use you to stand and confront the spirit of the age?

THE ORIGINAL DARK TOWER

FOCUS POINT

Genesis 11:4 says, "And they said, 'Come, let us build ourselves a city, and a tower whose top is in the heavens; *let us make a name for ourselves, lest we be scattered* abroad over the face of the whole earth.'" There are two significant things in this verse. First, we see that they wanted to make a name for themselves. Second, they did not want to be scattered abroad. In the natural, their population was continually growing, and the inevitable outcome would be that they would be scattered around the globe. This was one of God's commandments to Adam and Eve: to be fruitful, multiply, fill the earth, and subdue it (*see* Genesis 1:28). When people decide to go against God, the results are a devised plan that goes against God's plan. In Genesis 11:4, the plan was to make a name for themselves. They wanted notoriety and fame. They were saying, "Our way is better than God's way." Interestingly, God did exactly what they didn't want. Genesis 11:8 says, "So the LORD scattered them abroad from there over the face of all the earth, and they ceased building the city."

The Lord knows what is best for us. Have there been times in your life when you thought your own plan was better? Perhaps you were aware of God's plan for your life, but it didn't align with your desires. It's important to be honest with yourself. If you find yourself in that situation now, take a moment to ask the Lord for forgiveness and reposition yourself on the path He has called you to follow. If this doesn't apply to you, use this opportunity to thank God for the plans and purposes He has in store for you. Consider writing down your thoughts and prayers.

LUCIFER HAD HIGH AMBITION

Read Genesis 11:4 and Isaiah 14:14. In what ways do you see similarities in the responses of Nimrod and Lucifer?

WEAPONIZED PAWNS

In the book of Revelation, when Jesus calls out the seven churches, He says, "He who has an ear, let him hear what the Spirit is saying to the churches." This means that we can have ears that hear the Spirit and ears that don't. We see that Nimrod and his followers had ears to hear what the enemy was saying. They became pawns to darkness. Let's ensure our ears are attuned to the Holy Spirit and continually allow Him to speak truth to us, keeping us on the right path.

THE ANTI-ADAM

Nimrod lived up to his name, which meant *we rebel*. He led a rebellion against God and His plans. Have you ever thought about the significance of names? Look up your name and write its meaning. If you can't find it, ask the Lord to speak to you about who He sees you to be and the significance of your name.

CERN AND THE LARGE HADRON COLLIDER

In Genesis, God creates heaven and earth, the universe, and everything in it. Man has tried to disprove this throughout history. The devil is not a creator; he's a copier. He mimics and makes counterfeits. Modern creations such as CERN are believed by a growing number of people to be nefarious in its purposes. Although it may one day prove itself to not be a device of high evil, there are certainly enough questions that point to something dark taking place. In what ways would it seem that CERN or other modern scientific operations might be attempting to take similar actions against God and His creation?

OPENING A PORTAL

According to Stephen Hawking, what are the alleged dangers of CERN trying to open portals into another realm? What are your thoughts on the actions of CERN and what some find as a possible comparison to the verses in Revelation, particularly regarding the abyss or bottomless pit?

After reading through the nine points of interest involving CERN's origins and alleged agenda, list some things you were unaware of that stood out. How should the Church pray against these types of scientific schemes that contradict God's will? Write your prayer.

PARALLELS BETWEEN CERN AND THE TOWER OF BABEL

PERSONAL REFLECTIONS

As long as the *Ekklesia* is on earth, the gates of hell cannot prevail. The Church must assert its God-given authority and push back darkness and its schemes. It is not the time to draw back. God takes no pleasure in that. We need to rise, shine, and be all God has called us to be, no matter what the ungodly are doing.

Take this time for personal reflection to pray for the leaders in your city, state, and the United States. The body of Christ can pray out wicked leaders and pray for those hand-picked by God to do His work. Let's stand together in faith and cancel the assignment that entities like CERN might be attempting to bring forth in the form of what some believe is opening portals and possibly the abyss. Let's push back on all activity that agrees with an Antichrist spirit by faith and prayer.

CHAPTER THREE

Demon Forces, Civic Insanity, and Western Spirituality

SCRIPTURES

1. **First John 1:1-2**—That which was from the beginning, which we have heard, which we have seen with our eyes, which we have looked upon, and our hands have handled, concerning the Word of life— [2] the life was manifested, and we have seen, and bear witness, and declare to you that eternal life which was with the Father and was manifested to us.

2. **Ephesians 6:12**—For we do not wrestle against flesh and blood, but against principalities, against powers, against the rulers of the darkness of this age, against spiritual hosts of wickedness in the heavenly places.

3. **Acts 19:13-15**—Then some of the itinerant Jewish exorcists took it upon themselves to call the name of the Lord Jesus over those who had evil spirits, saying, "We exorcise you by the Jesus whom Paul preaches." [14] Also there were seven sons of Sceva, a Jewish chief priest, who did so. [15] And the evil spirit answered and said, "Jesus I know, and Paul I know; but who are you?"

4. **Romans 4:19-24 NIV**—Without weakening in his faith, he faced the fact that his body was as good as dead—since he was about a hundred years old—and that Sarah's womb was also dead. [20] Yet he did not waver through unbelief regarding the promise of God, but was strengthened in his faith and gave glory to God, [21] being ***fully persuaded*** that God had power to do what he had promised. [22] This is why "it was credited to him as righteousness." [23] The words "it was credited to him" were

written not for him alone, [24] but also for us, to whom God will credit righteousness—for us who believe in him who raised Jesus our Lord from the dead.

5. **John 4:24**—God is a Spirit, and those who worship Him must worship in spirit and truth.

6. **John 17:17**—Sanctify them by Your truth. Your word is truth.

7. **Second Corinthians 6:14**—Do not be unequally yoked together with unbelievers. For what fellowship has righteousness with lawlessness? And what communion has light with darkness?

8. **First John 1:5**—This is the message which we have heard from Him and declare to you, that God is light and in Him is no darkness at all.

9. **John 1:14**—And the Word became flesh and dwelt among us, and we beheld His glory, the glory as of the only begotten of the Father, full of grace and truth.

10. **Second Peter 1:3**—As His divine power has given to us all things that pertain to life and godliness, through the knowledge of Him who called us by glory and virtue.

11. **John 10:10**—The thief does not come except to steal, and to kill, and to destroy. I have come that they may have life, and that they may have it more abundantly.

RIGHTLY DISCERNING THE SPIRIT AND THE NATURAL

Similar to John the Revelator's day, we live in a world that often fosters strange teachings about Jesus. Unfortunately, many will believe various teachings on social media and popular culture rather than the truth of the Word of God. With this understanding, how should the Church address these matters in a proper way that will bring life, not confusion?

____

____

____

____

____

____

____

COMPREHENDING SPIRITUAL MATTERS WITH WESTERN MINDS

During the early Christian era, Gnosticism and Docetism were doctrinal heresies that deceived many. What are some false religions that are doing the same thing and deceiving many today?

MASS IGNORANCE OF DARK SPIRITUAL FORCES

Based on Paul Harvey's warning to America, what are your thoughts on the reality of what he is saying? Do you see this idea playing out today? If so, in what ways is this happening?

POWER OF THE CHURCH

The *Ekklesia* is a powerful force against the darkness and nefarious works of the enemy. Joseph lists a few things that the Church must do to hold back wickedness. In what ways can you play a role in this specific assignment?

CIVIC INSANITY

Throughout the years, we have seen groups of people wreak havoc in our nation. Things ranging from pandemics, election interference, border crisis, riots, and the expectation of more chaos to come. Individuals cooperating with a spirit of rebellion are blind and need a spiritual awakening. Take this time to pray for them to wake up and take their place in God's plan for them.

NAVIGATING SPIRITUAL WARFARE

FOCUS POINT

One of the biggest threats to the kingdom of darkness is when a believer knows who they are in Christ and the authority He has given them. This type of Christian will not back down. They will stand in full force against the enemy and see victory every time.

Jesus has equipped every believer with the tools they need to be an overcomer and a victor. Reading, meditating, and memorizing the Word is where a warrior is developed. Take this time to get into the Word. Search some scriptures that you can use when the enemy comes to attack. Write down a few.

DEMON FORCES ARE VILE

That at the name of Jesus every knee should bow, of those in heaven, and of those on earth, and of those under the earth, [11] and that every tongue should confess that Jesus Christ is Lord, to the glory of God the Father.

—Philippians 2:10-11

Knowing that the devil and his evil demonic hordes will have to bow down and confess that Jesus is Lord, how does this thought encourage you, knowing they will be defeated foes and must confess it with their mouths?

MY DEMONIC ENCOUNTERS AT A YOUNG AGE

Many people have experienced similar situations to those Joseph experienced during his youth. Unfortunately, many people are unaware of what is happening and the reasons behind it. Have you ever experienced a demonic or spiritual encounter? If so, what was the situation, and how did you navigate through it? Also, what would you advise a person you know who might be experiencing a demonic encounter?

FREE MORAL AGENTS

The sons of Sceva did not have a revelation of who Jesus was. This lack of understanding caused them to face extreme embarrassment and humiliation. Knowing that their formula-based exorcism attempt caused a reality check, why do you think it is crucial for the individual to have a revelation of Jesus?

ARE YOU FULLY PERSUADED?

Abraham was fully persuaded that God had the power to bring forth a son to him and Sarah. This scenario seemed impossible because they were both close to 100 years old and beyond childbearing age. God wants the "impossible" situations in your life to become possible. The Lord desires you to be fully persuaded in your heart that He has the power to do what He has promised for you. Take this time to thank God for His promises, which are yes and amen!

GOD AND THE DEVIL ARE IN A TERRITORY WAR FOR YOUR MIND

What are some practical ways to give your mind to God and strengthen your beliefs in Him, as opposed to being led by the influences of the devil?

DARKNESS MAY WALK OVER BUT IT WILL GO LIMPING BACK

Sometimes, the biggest battle a believer faces is the one within their mind. The enemy is aware of this and works diligently to occupy as much space in your thoughts as possible. Is this something you've experienced in your life? Have you encountered a mind battle that you managed to overcome? What steps did you take to achieve victory in that area?

GOD AND THE DEVIL ARE NOT BUSINESS PARTNERS

How does the concept of being "unequally yoked" in 2 Corinthians 6:14 relate to the idea of light and darkness in a believer's life?

ONGOING GOOD TEACHING IS THE BEST FORM OF DELIVERANCE

PERSONAL REFLECTIONS

There is a teaching that suggests, "If you are facing trials, if you are sick, or if you are hurting in some way, God is trying to teach you something." Another similar idea is, "You must have done something wrong to be going through this trial; it must be God's will for you to endure this." These notions can be very dangerous and harmful. As stated in John 10:10, *the thief comes to steal, kill, and destroy*. It does not say that God does these things. Instead, it emphasizes that God offers life and that we may have it more abundantly. God does not bring sickness, hardships, or trials to teach us lessons; He brings abundant life.

Take a moment to reflect on what John 10:10 means to you and envision what an abundant life looks like for a believer. If you have believed in the harmful teachings mentioned at the beginning of this reflection, take time to repent and ask the Lord for a deeper understanding of what He has prepared for you. Write down your thoughts or prayers.

CHAPTER FOUR

Power of the Air and Breaking the Rebellion of Witchcraft

SCRIPTURES

1. **Ephesians 2:2**—In which you once walked according to the course of this world, according to the prince of the power of the air, the spirit who now works in the sons of disobedience.

2. **Daniel 10:10-14**—Suddenly, a hand touched me, which made me tremble on
my knees and on the palms of my hands. [11] And he said to me, "O Daniel, man
greatly beloved, understand the words that I speak to you, and stand upright, for I
have now been sent to you." While he was speaking this word to me, I stood trem-
bling. [12] Then he said to me, "Do not fear, Daniel, for from the first day that you set
your heart to understand, and to humble yourself before your God, your words were
heard; and I have come because of your words. [13] But the prince of the kingdom of
Persia withstood me twenty-one days; and behold, Michael, one of the chief princes,
came to help me, for I had been left alone there with the kings of Persia. [14] Now I
have come to make you understand what will happen to your people in the latter
days, for the vision refers to many days yet to come."

3. **Hosea 4:6**—My people are destroyed for lack of knowledge. Because you have rejected knowledge, I also will reject you from being priest for Me; because you have forgotten the law of your God, I also will forget your children.

4. **John 14:30 KJV**—Hereafter I will not talk much with you: for the prince of this world cometh, and hath nothing in me.

5. **John 12:31 KJV**—Now is the judgment of this world: now shall the prince of this world be cast out.

6. **Ephesians 2:1-3**—And you He ***made alive,*** who were dead in trespasses and sins, [2] in which you ***once walked*** according to the course of this world, according to the prince of the power of the air, the spirit who now works in the sons of disobedience,[3] among whom also we all once conducted ourselves in the lusts of our flesh, fulfilling the desires of the flesh and of the mind, and were by nature children of wrath, just as the others.

7. **Numbers 33:52**—Then you shall drive out all the inhabitants of the land from before you, destroy all their engraved stones, destroy all their molded images, and demolish all their ***high places***.

8. **Deuteronomy 12:2**—You shall utterly destroy all the places where the nations which you shall dispossess served their gods, on the ***high mountains*** and on the hills and under every green tree.

9. **Second Corinthians 10:5**—Casting down arguments and every ***high thing*** that exalts itself against the knowledge of God, bringing every thought into captivity to the obedience of Christ.

10. **First Peter 5:8**—Be sober, be vigilant; because your adversary the devil walks about like a roaring lion, seeking whom he may devour.

11. **Romans 14:17**—For the kingdom of God is not eating and drinking, but righteousness and peace and joy in the Holy Spirit.

12. **Romans 12:2**—And do not be conformed to this world, but be transformed by the renewing of your mind, that you may prove what is that good and acceptable and perfect will of God.

13. **First Corinthians 13:9-10, 12**—For we know in part and we prophesy in part. [10] But when that which is perfect has come, then that which is in part will be done away.... [12] For now we see in a ***mirror, dimly,*** but then face to face. Now I know in part, but then I shall know just as I also am known.

14. **Hebrews 5:14**—...That is, those who by reason of use have their senses exercised to discern both good and evil.

15. **Ephesians 6:12**—For we do not wrestle against flesh and blood, but against principalities, against powers, against the rulers of the darkness of this age, against spiritual hosts of wickedness in the heavenly places.

16. **First Samuel 15:22-23**—So Samuel said: "Has the Lord as great delight in burnt offerings and sacrifices, as in obeying the voice of the Lord? Behold, to obey is better than sacrifice, and to heed than the fat of rams. [23] For rebellion is as the sin of witchcraft, and stubbornness is as iniquity and idolatry. Because you have rejected the word of the LORD, He also has rejected you from being king."

17. **First Samuel 28:3-21**—Now ***Samuel had died***, and all Israel had lamented for him and buried him in Ramah, in his own city. And Saul had put the mediums and the spiritists out of the land. [4] Then the Philistines gathered together, and came and encamped at Shunem. So Saul gathered all Israel together, and they encamped at Gilboa. [5] ***When Saul saw the army of the Philistines, he was afraid, and his heart trembled greatly.*** [6] ***And when Saul inquired of the Lord, the Lord did not answer him, either by dreams or by Urim or by the prophets.*** [7] ***Then Saul said to his servants, "Find me a woman who is a medium, that I may go to her and inquire of her." And his servants said to him, "In fact, there is a woman who is a medium at En Dor."*** [8] So Saul disguised himself and put on other clothes, and he went, and two men with him; and they came to the woman by night. And he said, ***"Please conduct a séance for me, and bring up for me the one I shall name to you."*** [9] Then the woman said to him, "Look, you know what Saul has done, how he has cut off the mediums and the spiritists from the land. Why then do you lay a snare for my life, to cause me to die?" [10] And Saul swore to her by the Lord, saying, "As the Lord lives, no punishment shall come upon you for this thing." [11] Then the woman said, "Whom shall I bring up for you?" And he said, "Bring up Samuel for me." [12] ***When the woman saw Samuel, she cried out with a loud voice. And the woman spoke to Saul, saying, "Why have you deceived me? For you are Saul!"*** [13] And the king said to her, "Do not be afraid. What did you see?" And the woman said to Saul, "I saw a spirit ascending out of the earth." [14] So he said to her, "What is his form?" And she said, "An old man is coming up, and he is covered with a mantle." And Saul perceived that it was Samuel, and he stooped with his face to the ground and bowed down. [15] ***Now Samuel said to Saul, "Why have you disturbed me by bringing me up?"*** And Saul answered, "I am deeply distressed; for the Philistines make war against me, and God has departed from me and does not answer me anymore, neither by prophets nor by dreams. Therefore I have called you, that you may reveal to me what I should do." [16] Then Samuel said:

"So why do you ask me, seeing the Lord has departed from you and has become your enemy? [17] And the Lord has done for Himself as He spoke by me. For the Lord has torn the kingdom out of your hand and given it to your neighbor, David. [18] Because you did not obey the voice of the Lord nor execute His fierce wrath upon Amalek, therefore the Lord has done this thing to you this day. [19] Moreover the Lord will also deliver Israel with you into the hand of the Philistines. And tomorrow you and your sons will be with me. The Lord will also deliver the army of Israel into the hand of the Philistines." [20] Immediately Saul fell full length on the ground, and was dreadfully afraid because of the words of Samuel. And there was no strength in him, for he had eaten no food all day or all night. [21] And the woman came to Saul and saw that he was severely troubled, and said to him, "Look, your maidservant has obeyed your voice, and I have put my life in my hands and heeded the words which you spoke to me."

18. **Galatians 1:8**—But even if we, or an ***angel from heaven***, preach any other gospel to you than what we have preached to you, let him be accursed.

19. **Romans 12:1**—I beseech you therefore, brethren, by the mercies of God, that you present your bodies a living sacrifice, holy, acceptable to God, which is your reasonable service.

What allows the devil to operate freely in this world, and why is it essential to keep the mind aligned with the Word to prevent the devil from gaining influence?

____

____

____

____

____

____

____

____

____

____

DIFFERENCES BETWEEN THE OLD AND NEW TESTAMENT

There are numerous differences between the Old and New Testaments. List some of the differences that you have come across through your reading.

DIFFICULTIES WITH PRINCIPALITIES

The main difference between the Old and New Testaments is Jesus! He is the game changer in every situation. Not only did Jesus make a way for our salvation, He also left us the Holy Spirit, who lives within us. The Holy Spirit is always present, hears our prayers, and teaches us how to pray. Take a moment to thank the Lord for the gift of the Holy Spirit.

PRINCE OF THIS WORLD BEING CAST OUT

Many people have surrendered themselves to the devil and his lies. What they may not realize is that they don't have to succumb to this. They can be freed from the enemy's grip and achieve victory. With this in mind, why do you believe that preaching the gospel is the most powerful form of spiritual warfare? How can you contribute to the bigger picture of helping those bound by the devil to be set free?

WHAT ABOUT THE PRINCE OF THE POWER OF THE AIR?

FOCUS POINT

Or do you not know that as many of us as were baptized into Christ Jesus were baptized into His death? [4] Therefore we were buried with Him through baptism into death, that just as Christ was raised from the dead by the glory of the Father, even so we also should walk in newness of life. [5] For if we have been united together in the likeness of His death, certainly we also shall be in the likeness of His resurrection, [6] knowing this, that our old man was crucified with Him, that the body of sin might be done away with, that we should no longer be slaves of sin. [7] For he who has died has been freed from sin. [8] Now if we died with Christ, we believe that we shall also live with Him, [9] knowing that Christ, having been raised from the dead, dies no more. Death no longer has dominion over Him. [10] For the death that He died, He died to sin once for all; but the life that He lives, He lives to God. [11] Likewise you also, reckon yourselves to be dead indeed to sin, but alive to God in Christ Jesus our Lord.

—Romans 6:3-11

Ephesians 2:1-3 and Romans 6:3-11 emphasize that those who are born again and baptized are freed from their trespasses and sins and made alive to God. There is great significance in confessing with the mouth that Jesus is Lord, professing one's faith before others, and being baptized.

Using this focus point, please write a brief testimony about your salvation. If you have not yet made Jesus the Lord of your life or been baptized, there is a salvation prayer at the end of Chapter Thirteen. If you prayed this prayer for the first time, please contact our office at info@zministries.com. Our team would be happy to send you our free teaching, *Saved: Rescued for a Purpose.* God bless!

HIGH PLACES

What issues arise from the interpretation that associates high places with physical locations in spiritual warfare?

TWO GREEK WORDS; TWO DIFFERENT MEANINGS

How does understanding the meanings of the two Greek words for "air" help clarify the context in which the devil and his minions operate?

MIND CONTROL

Whoever controls the mind, the thinking process, controls the direction people go. Why do you think this is true? What does Romans 12:2 instruct us to do concerning the mind?

THE MIRROR AND YOUR SENSES

The soul is made of your mind, will, and emotions. Why is it so important to keep these under control and not to let your emotions run away and direct the course of your life?

DEMONS' UNAUTHORIZED POWER

Many have given the devil complete control over their lives. Because of this, we, as believers, will come into contact with these types of people and need to be prepared. Our presence should demand an explanation. In what ways should the believer be ready for this type of encounter?

REBELLION AS WITCHCRAFT

In today's world, it is often encouraged to be rebellious. It is as if the world is creating the mindset that good is bad and evil is good. Have you seen this type of mindset being taught in our world? If so, list some examples of what you are seeing.

VIOLATION OF AUTHORITY

Why do you think it's an act of rebellion when a person puts their will over God's will?

THE WITCH OF ENDOR

What started with disobedience turned into full rebellion through the practice of witchcraft. How do you think someone gets to this point?

UNAUTHORIZED ACCESS TO THE REALM OF THE SPIRIT

One of the definitions for the word "witchcraft" from the Merriam-Webster Dictionary is *an irresistible influence or fascination.*[1] Fake encounters, self-deception, and demonic encounters have a connection to this specific definition. Write your thoughts on what that connection is.

HOW SHOULD THE BELIEVER RESPOND?

PERSONAL REFLECTIONS

For God has not given us a spirit of fear, but of power and of love and of a ***sound mind.***

—2 Timothy 1:7

For the Spirit God gave us does not make us timid, but gives us power, love, and ***self-discipline.***

—2 Timothy 1:7 NIV

Second Timothy 1:7 is a reminder that God does not give the spirit of fear or timidity. Instead, He gives power, love, and a sound mind; or as the NIV says, self-discipline.

When you discipline yourself, you can overcome all things, especially fear, that the enemy throws your way. Self-discipline involves keeping your mind focused on the Word of God. When thoughts come to bring you down or discourage you, it is your responsibility to take captive those thoughts by speaking the Word of God.

Read Psalm 139:23-24. Write these verses down and request that God reveal to you the issues He sees that need to be addressed. Take notes on what you hear, and spend focused time with the Holy Spirit.

SECTION TWO

Strategies of the Devil and the Responsibilities of the Believer

CHAPTER FIVE

SATAN'S RAGE

SCRIPTURES

1. **Revelation 12:12**—Therefore rejoice, O heavens, and you who dwell in them! Woe to the inhabitants of the earth and the sea! For the devil has come down to you, having great wrath, because he knows that he has a short time.

2. **Ezekiel 28:14**—You were the anointed cherub who covers; I established you; you were on the holy mountain of God; you walked back and forth in the midst of fiery stones.

3. **Isaiah 14:12-15**—How you are fallen from heaven, O Lucifer, son of the morning! How you are cut down to the ground, you who weakened the nations! [13] For you have said in your heart: "I will ascend into heaven, I will exalt my throne above the stars of God; I will also sit on the mount of the congregation on the farthest sides of the north; [14] I will ascend above the heights of the clouds, I will be like the Most High." [15] Yet you shall be brought down to Sheol, to the lowest depths of the Pit.

4. **John 16:11**—Of judgment, because the ruler of this world is judged.

5. **John 8:44**—You are of your father the devil, and the desires of your father you want to do. He was **a *murderer from the beginning***, and does not stand in the truth, because there is no truth in him. When he speaks a lie, he speaks from his own resources, ***for he is a liar and the father of it***.

6. **Revelation 12:9**—So the great dragon was cast out, that serpent of old, called the Devil and Satan, who deceives the whole world; he was cast to the earth, and his angels were cast out with him.

7. **Revelation 20:2**—He laid hold of the dragon, that serpent of old, who is the Devil and Satan, and bound him for a thousand years.

8. **Job 1:6**—Now there was a day when the ***sons of God*** came to present themselves before the Lord, and Satan also came among them.

9. **Job 38:7**—When the morning stars sang together, and all ***the sons of God*** shouted for joy?

10. **Revelation 12:17**—And the dragon was enraged with the woman, and he went to make war with the rest of her offspring, who keep the commandments of God and have the testimony of Jesus Christ.

11. **First Corinthians 6:2-3**—Do you not know that the saints will judge the world? And if the world will be judged by you, are you unworthy to judge the smallest matters? [3] Do you not know that we shall judge angels? How much more, things that pertain to this life?

12. **Jude 1:6**—And the angels who did not keep their proper domain, but left their own abode, He has reserved in everlasting chains under darkness for the judgment of the great day.

13. **Ezekiel 28:13-19**—***You were in Eden***, the garden of God; every precious stone was your covering: the sardius, topaz, and diamond, beryl, onyx, and jasper, sapphire, turquoise, and emerald with gold. The workmanship of your timbrels and pipes was prepared for you on the day you were created. [14] You were the anointed cherub who covers; I established you; you were on the holy mountain of God; ***you walked back and forth in the midst of fiery stones***. [15] You were perfect in your ways from the day you were created, till iniquity was found in you. [16] ***By the abundance of your trading*** you became filled with violence within, and you sinned; therefore I cast you as a profane thing out of the mountain of God; and I destroyed you, O covering cherub, from the midst of the fiery stones. [17] Your heart was lifted up because of your beauty; you corrupted your wisdom for the sake of your splendor; I cast you to the ground, I laid you before kings, that they might gaze at you. [18] You defiled your sanctuaries by the multitude of your iniquities, by the iniquity of your trading; therefore I brought fire from your midst; it devoured you, and I turned you to ashes upon the earth in the sight of all who saw you. [19] All who knew you among the peoples are astonished at you; you have become a horror, and shall be no more forever.

14. **Luke 10:18-19**—And He said to them, "I saw Satan fall like lightning from heaven. [19] Behold, I give you the authority to trample on serpents and scorpions, and over all the power of the enemy, and nothing shall by any means hurt you."

15. **John 3:1-6**—There was a man of the Pharisees named Nicodemus, a ruler of the Jews. [2] This man came to Jesus by night and said to Him, "Rabbi, we know that You are a teacher come from God; for no one can do these signs that You do unless God is with him." [3] Jesus answered and said to him, "Most assuredly, I say to you, unless one is born again, he cannot see the Kingdom of God." [4] Nicodemus said to Him, "How can a man be born when he is old? Can he enter a second time into his mother's womb and be born?" [5] Jesus answered, "Most assuredly, I say to you, ***unless one is born of water and the Spirit, he cannot enter the kingdom of God***. [6] That which is born of the flesh is flesh, and that which is born of the Spirit is spirit."

16. **Genesis 3:15**—And I will put enmity between you and the woman, and between your seed and her Seed; He shall bruise your head, and you shall bruise His heel.

17. **John 20:22**—And when He had said this, He breathed on them, and said to them, "Receive the Holy Spirit."

18. **Romans 8:1-4**—There is therefore now no condemnation to those who are in Christ Jesus, who do not walk according to the flesh, but according to the Spirit. [2] For the law of the Spirit of life in Christ Jesus has made me free from the law of sin and death. [3] For what the law could not do in that it was weak through the flesh, God did by sending His own Son in the likeness of sinful flesh, on account of sin: He condemned sin in the flesh, [4] that the righteous requirement of the law might be fulfilled in us who do not walk according to the flesh but according to the Spirit.

The devil has great wrath against humankind. The definition of "wrath" is *strong, vengeful anger or indignation*,[1] and this is what the devil carries. He cares nothing for humanity. He wants to take as many to hell with him as possible. This is why it is crucial to be vigilant and prepared to minister to those around us, to snatch people from his grasp, and expose them to the light. Let's be willing vessels!

LUCIFER'S FALL

Arrogance, pride, and ambition were characteristics found in Lucifer, which ultimately led to his expulsion from the presence of God. People are not exempt from experiencing these same traits. How can a believer avoid succumbing to such temptations and emotions?

LUCIFER'S CONTEMPT

In John 8:44, Jesus refers to the devil as "the father of lies." He was able to persuade angels in heaven to believe his lies instead of the truth of God. Today, Lucifer continues to lead people away from the truth found in the Word of God and God Himself. Why do you think those particular angels and people are so quick to listen to the voice of a liar rather than the Voice of God?

What are your thoughts on 1 Corinthians 6:3 and the idea that we will judge angels?

____

____

____

____

____

____

____

____

____

____

____

____

____

KEEP THE WORD OF GOD THE MAIN THING

FOCUS POINT

Luke 10:18-19 states, "And He said to them, 'I saw Satan fall like lightning from heaven. [19] Behold, I give you the authority to trample on serpents and scorpions, and over all the power of the enemy, and nothing shall by any means hurt you.'"

It's important to note that Jesus observed Satan's fall from heaven. Have you ever seen a meteor enter the Earth's atmosphere and impact the planet? The force of such an event can create a large crater. Now, imagine the devil falling with that same intensity and the impact it had on him. He likely experienced pain and humiliation for his evil actions.

Jesus' words remind us that the devil is a defeated foe. Because of this defeat, we have the power to trample on serpents and scorpions. Nothing can harm us because the devil has been cast out of heaven! He has lost, and as a result, we can achieve victory in all areas of our lives. Praise God for Jesus!

THOSE BORN OF WATER HAVE AUTHORITY

Why was it important for Jesus to be born of water? Why is it vital for a person to be born of water and the Spirit to enter the kingdom of God?

WHAT TOOK SO LONG?

Prophecies had to be documented, communicated, and embraced for Jesus to be born. Provide a list of prophecies that refer to the coming Messiah. If you are not already familiar with any, make it a priority to research some now.

BORN OF THE SPIRIT

Those who are born of water and the Spirit are free from condemnation. Jesus has brought us life and set us free from the law of sin and death. His death on the cross has paved the way for us to live righteously, knowing that through Him, we can follow the Spirit rather than the desires of the flesh. In what ways do you seek to embrace this freedom and walk according to the Spirit?

ONE BELIEVER IS ENOUGH TO ROUT THE FORCES OF HELL

PERSONAL REFLECTIONS

Even on a bad day, you are anointed to be the very best there is! God has equipped you to overcome every scheme that the enemy throws your way. You are destined for victory. Having a physical body, being baptized, and being filled with the Holy Spirit set you apart from the devil and evil spirits.

It is crucial for you to understand this and gain a revelation of what you carry. How can recognizing your authority in Christ change the way you approach spiritual challenges and resist negative thoughts or attacks?

CHAPTER SIX

CONQUERING THE DEVIL'S GAMES

SCRIPTURES

1. **Luke 10:18 KJV**—And He said unto them, I beheld Satan as lightning fall from heaven.

2. **First John 3:8**—He who sins is of the devil, for the devil has sinned from the beginning. For this purpose the Son of God was manifested, that He might destroy the works of the devil.

3. **John 10:10**—The thief does not come except to steal, and to kill, and to destroy. I have come that they may have life, and that they may have it more abundantly.

4. **Hebrews 2:14**—Inasmuch then as the children have partaken of flesh and blood, He Himself likewise shared in the same, that through death He might destroy him who had the power of death, that is, the devil.

5. **John 12:31**—Now is the judgment of this world; now the ruler of this world will be cast out.

6. **John 14:30**—I will no longer talk much with you, for the ruler of this world is coming, and he has nothing in Me.

7. **Colossians 2:15**—Having disarmed principalities and powers, He made a ***public spectacle*** of them, triumphing over them in it.

8. **Luke 10:19**—Behold, I give you the authority to trample on serpents and scorpions, and over all the power of the enemy, and nothing shall by any means hurt you.

9. **Second Corinthians 11:3**—But I fear, lest somehow, as the serpent deceived Eve by his craftiness, so your minds may be corrupted from the simplicity that is in Christ.

10. **John 15:5**—I am the vine, you are the branches. He who abides in Me, and I in him, bears much fruit; for without Me you can do nothing.

11. **Second Corinthians 11:2-4 NLT**—For I am jealous for you with the jealousy of God himself. I promised you as a pure bride to one husband—Christ. [3] But I fear that somehow your pure and undivided devotion to Christ will be corrupted, just as Eve was deceived by the cunning ways of the serpent. [4] You happily put up with whatever anyone tells you, even if they preach a different Jesus than the one we preach, or a different kind of Spirit than the one you received, or a different kind of gospel than the one you believed.

12. **Second Corinthians 2:10-11**—Now whom you forgive anything, I also forgive. For if indeed I have forgiven anything, I have forgiven that one for your sakes in the presence of Christ, [11] lest Satan should take advantage of us; for we are not ignorant of his devices.

13. **Matthew 18:22**—Jesus said to him, "I do not say to you, up to seven times, but up to seventy times seven."

14. **First Peter 5:8**—Be sober, be vigilant; because your adversary the devil walks about like a roaring lion, seeking whom he may devour.

15. **Genesis 1:26**—Then God said, "Let Us make man in Our image, according to Our likeness; let them have dominion over the fish of the sea, over the birds of the air, and over the cattle, over all the earth and over every creeping thing that creeps on the earth."

16. **Psalm 8:5**—For You have made him a little lower than the ***angels***, and You have crowned him with glory and honor.

17. **Psalm 8:5 NASB**—Yet You have made him a little lower than ***God,*** and You crown him with glory and majesty!

18. **Second Corinthians 6:18**—I will be a Father to you, and you shall be My sons and daughters, says the Lord Almighty.

19. **Ephesians 2:5-6**—Even when we were dead in trespasses, [He] made us alive together with Christ (by grace you have been saved), [6] and raised us up together, and made us sit together in the heavenly places in Christ Jesus.

20. **First John 4:17**—Love has been perfected among us in this: that we may have boldness in the day of judgment; because as He is, so are we in this world.

21. **Romans 8:17**—And if children, then heirs—heirs of God and joint heirs with Christ, if indeed we suffer with Him, that we may also be glorified together.

22. **John 15:15**—No longer do I call you servants, for a servant does not know what his master is doing; but I have called you friends, for all things that I heard from My Father I have made known to you.

23. **Luke 10:19**—Behold, I give you the authority to trample on serpents and scorpions, and over all the power of the enemy, and nothing shall by any means hurt you.

24. **Romans 8:29**—For whom He foreknew, He also predestined to be conformed to the image of His Son, that He might be the firstborn among many brethren.

There is a faulty teaching that says God lets the devil attack believers. Some even go as far as saying that God will tell the devil how to attack, such as bringing sickness and disease on someone. According to 2 Corinthians 6:14, which says, "Do not be unequally yoked together with unbelievers. For what fellowship has righteousness with lawlessness? *And what communion has light with darkness*?" How does this verse contradict this false teaching?

____

____

____

____

____

____

____

JESUS FULFILLED HIS PURPOSE

John 16:33 says, "These things I have spoken to you, that in Me you may have peace. In the world you will have tribulation; but be of good cheer, I have overcome the world." Jesus has overcome every evil thing in the world; because of this, we too can overcome. Thank the Lord for Jesus!

JESUS PUNISHED THE DARK POWERS

FOCUS POINT

Isaiah 6:1: "In the year that King Uzziah died, I saw the lord high and exalted, seated on a throne, and the train of his robe filled the temple." The imagery is taken from the practice of earthly kings. The great monarchs of Egypt and Assyria owned elaborate thrones. These great monarchs commonly wore flowing robes. It told how powerful the king was in that particular country.

As a king defeated the camp of another king, he would cut off the defeated king's train and sew it onto his train. Eventually, this train became longer and more glorious as he was the obvious victor from many battles.

Solomon's throne was perhaps even grander than any of these, as mentioned in 1 Kings 10:18-20. It was placed at the summit of "six steps" so that its occupant was "high and lifted up" above all his courtiers. His train, "the skirts of his robe," began to occupy his temple.

God is seated on the throne...high and lifted up—and his train—the glory of the Lord fills the temple.

What great comfort there is in knowing Jesus has already defeated the enemy, and we don't need to struggle! It's a powerful thought that He's there to protect and defend us.[1]

THE DEVIL'S ALLOWED ACCESS

Having a corrupted mind means that the devil has been given access and has deceived it. How did the devil deceive Eve by his craftiness? What does that look like?

ABIDE IN JESUS

John 15:1-4 says, "I am the true vine, and My Father is the vinedresser. [2] Every branch in Me that does not bear fruit He takes away; and every branch that bears fruit He prunes, that it may bear more fruit. [3] You are already clean because of the word which I have spoken to you. [4] Abide in Me, and I in you. As the branch cannot bear fruit of itself, unless it abides in the vine, neither can you, unless you abide in Me." We must abide in Jesus. He desires us to bear much fruit. According to John 15:5, what is an important revelation we need to know so that we produce good and abundant fruit?

FORGIVENESS OUTFLANKS OFFENSE

Why do you think that offense and unforgiveness allow the devil to have a foothold in your mind?

MIND GAMES

Forgiveness and love are powerful weapons against the devil. Unfortunately, many people have fallen victim to destructive thoughts and situations, such as the example of a potentially harmful conversation. Have you ever faced a similar situation or experienced mind games like this? If so, please share your experience and the outcome.

PHYSICAL BODIES OUTRANK DEMON SPIRITS

PERSONAL REFLECTIONS

When you were born again, you became a child of God immediately. Some will try to discredit this based on your past or your current circumstances. That's not biblical. When you get saved, all your sins are wiped away and forgotten. God doesn't see a stain on you; He sees Jesus' blood covering you. This is why Ephesians 2:4-9 says, "But God, who is rich in mercy, because of His great love with which He loved us, [5] even when we were dead in trespasses, made us alive together with Christ (by grace you have been saved), [6] and raised us up together, and made us sit together in the heavenly places in Christ Jesus, [7] that in the ages to come He might show the exceeding riches of His grace in His kindness toward us in Christ Jesus. [8] For by grace you have been saved through faith, and that not of yourselves; it is the gift of God, [9] not of works, lest anyone should boast." You are not saved by what you do. You are saved by what He did on the cross.

Have you ever let your sins keep you from pursuing Jesus? Or, have you felt that because you might have messed up, Jesus is going to be mad at you? Sometimes, these mindsets can make us feel like we should get our affairs in order before coming to Jesus, but the opposite is true. When you are having a hard time or seem to be struggling with the same thing, this is when you need to pursue Jesus all the more. Take this time to seek the Lord, asking Him to reveal to you how He views you, regardless of your current stage. Let His words wash over you.

Write what you hear Him say.

____

____

____

____

____

____

____

CHAPTER SEVEN

THE BATTLE FOR YOUR MIND

SCRIPTURES

1. **Luke 4:1-4**—Then Jesus, being filled with the Holy Spirit, returned from the Jordan and was led by the Spirit into the wilderness, [2] being tempted for forty days by the devil. And in those days He ate nothing, and afterward, when they had ended, He was hungry. [3] And the devil said to Him, "If You are the Son of God, command this stone to become bread." [4] But Jesus answered him, saying, "It is written, 'Man shall not live by bread alone, but by every word of God.'"

2. **Genesis 3:1-4**—Now the serpent was more cunning than any beast of the field which the Lord God had made. And he said to the woman, "Has God indeed said, 'You shall not eat of every tree of the garden'?" [2] And the woman said to the serpent, "We may eat the fruit of the trees of the garden; [3] but of the fruit of the tree which is in the midst of the garden, God has said, 'You shall not eat it, nor shall you touch it, lest you die.' " [4] Then the serpent said to the woman, "You will not surely die."

3. **Luke 4:5-8**—Then the devil, taking Him up on a high mountain, showed Him all the kingdoms of the world in a moment of time. [6] And the devil said to Him, "All this authority I will give You, and their glory; for this has been delivered to me, and I give it to whomever I wish. [7] Therefore, if You will worship before me, all will be Yours." [8] And Jesus answered and said to him, "Get behind me Satan! For it is written 'You shall worship the Lord your God, and Him only you shall serve.'"

4. **Luke 4:9-11**—Then he brought Him to Jerusalem, set Him on the pinnacle of the temple, and said to Him, "If you are the Son of God, throw Yourself down from here. [10] **For it is written**: 'He shall give His angels charge over you, to keep you [11] and in their hands they shall bear you up lest you dash your foot against a stone.'"

5. **Luke 10:18**—And He said to them, "I saw Satan fall like lightning from heaven."

6. **Job 1:6**—Now there was a day when the sons of God came to present themselves before the Lord, and Satan also came among them.

7. **Job 1:7**—And the Lord said to Satan, "From where do you come?" So Satan answered the Lord and said, "From going to and fro on the earth, and from walking back and forth on it."

8. **Job 1:8-12**—Then the Lord said to Satan, "Have you considered My servant Job, that there is none like him on the earth, a blameless and upright man, one who fears God and shuns evil?" [9] So Satan answered the Lord and said, "Does Job fear God for nothing? [10] Have You not made a hedge around him, around his household, and around all that he has on every side? You have blessed the work of his hands, and his possessions have increased in the land. [11] But now, stretch out Your hand and touch all that he has, and he will surely curse You to Your face!" [12] And the Lord said to Satan, "***Behold***, all that he has is in your power; only do not lay a hand on his person." So Satan went out from the presence of the Lord.

9. **Proverbs 18:21**—Death and life are in the power of the tongue, and those who love it will eat its fruit.

10. **Luke 4:12-13**—And Jesus answered and said to him, "It has been said, 'You shall not tempt the Lord your God.'" [13] Now when the devil had ended every temptation, he departed from Him until an opportune time.

11. **Matthew 16:21-23**—From that time Jesus began to show to His disciples that He must go to Jerusalem, and suffer many things from the elders and chief priests and scribes, and be killed, and be raised the third day. [22] Then Peter took Him aside and began to rebuke Him, saying, "Far be it from You, Lord; this shall not happen to You!" [23] But He turned and said to Peter, "***Get behind Me, Satan! You are an offense to Me***, for you are not mindful of the things of God, but the things of men."

12. **Malachi 3:10**—"Bring all the tithes into the storehouse, that there may be food in My house, and try Me now in this," says the Lord of hosts, "If I will not open for you the windows of heaven and pour out for you such blessing that there will not be room enough to receive it."

13. **Acts 28:3-5**—But when Paul had gathered a bundle of sticks and laid them on the fire, a viper came out because of the heat, and fastened on his hand. [4] So when the natives saw the creature hanging from his hand, they said to one another, "No doubt this man is a murderer, whom, though he has escaped the sea, yet justice does not allow to live." [5] But he shook off the creature into the fire and suffered no harm.

14. **Luke 10:19**—Behold, I give you the authority to trample on serpents and scorpions, and over all the power of the enemy, and nothing shall by any means hurt you.

15. **John 3:5-7**—Jesus answered, "Most assuredly, I say to you, unless one is born of water and the Spirit, he cannot enter the kingdom of God. [6] That which is born of the flesh is flesh, and that which is born of the Spirit is spirit. [7] Do not marvel that I said to you, 'You must be born again.'"

16. **Revelation 12:10**—Then I heard a loud voice saying in heaven, "Now salvation, and strength, and the kingdom of our God, and the power of His Christ have come, for the accuser of our brethren, who accused them before our God day and night, has been cast down."

17. **Hebrews 7:25**—Therefore He is also able to save to the uttermost those who come to God through Him, since He always lives to make intercession for them.

18. **First John 4:17**—Love has been perfected among us in this: that we may have boldness in the day of judgment; because as He is, so are we in this world.

19. **First Peter 5:8**—Be sober, be vigilant; because your adversary the devil walks about like a roaring lion, seeking whom he may devour.

20. **Genesis 3:14**—So the Lord God said to the serpent: "Because you have done this, you are cursed more than all cattle, and more than every beast of the field; on your belly you shall go, and you shall eat dust all the days of your life."

21. **Genesis 3:19**—In the sweat of your face you shall eat bread till you return to the ground, for out of it you were taken; ***for dust you are,*** and to dust you shall return.

22. **Ephesians 6:16**—Above all, taking the shield of faith with which you will be able to quench all the fiery darts of the wicked one.

23. **Second Corinthians 10:5**—Casting down arguments and every high thing that exalts itself against the knowledge of God, bringing every thought into captivity to the obedience of Christ.

24. **Exodus 1:8**—Now there arose a new king over Egypt, who did not know Joseph.

25. **Philippians 4:7**—And the peace of God, which surpasses all understanding, will guard your hearts and minds through Christ Jesus.

26. **James 5:16-18**—...The effective, fervent prayer of a righteous man avails much.
[17] Elijah was a man with a nature like ours, and he prayed earnestly that it would not
rain; and it did not rain on the land for three years and six months. [18] And he prayed
again, and the heaven gave rain, and the earth produced its fruit.

27. **James 5:16 AMP**—...The heartfelt and persistent prayer of a righteous man (believer) can accomplish much [when put into action and made effective by God—it is dynamic and can have tremendous power].

28. **Proverbs 29:18**—Where there is no revelation, the people cast off restraint; but happy is he who keeps the law.

SATAN'S TEMPTATION OF JESUS

What are the best ways to learn the devil's tactics, and how will this knowledge assist you in spiritual warfare?

____

____

____

____

____

____

____

____

____

____

IT IS WRITTEN

The devil often assaults people's identities. It is no wonder that many believe the lie that who they were born isn't who they are supposed to be. In the culture today, in what ways do you see the enemy attacking identity?

THE DEVIL WAS OFFERING JESUS A SHORTCUT

The devil quoted scripture out of context, claiming that if Jesus were to throw Himself off the pinnacle of the temple, the angels would take charge over Him. While the devil is crafty, he lacks creativity and consistently seeks to distort the truth. Jesus understood the scripture the devil was referencing, which allowed Him to confidently respond, "It is written," knowing the truth of the Word.

It is crucial to know the Bible for these reasons: to be prepared when someone attempts to misquote or misinterpret it, enabling you to respond with an informed and accurate answer, just as Jesus did.

JOB'S TEMPTATION

How do we know that Satan had authority over the earth and could offer it to Jesus? Why do you think God reminded Satan of this authority by granting him access to Job?

A MORE OPPORTUNE TIME

The devil is on the lookout for a more opportune time to tempt individuals to give in to his plans. In the story of Matthew 16:21-23, how do you think Peter, as a disciple, was used by the devil to confront Jesus about His death and resurrection?

THERE IS ONLY ONE PLACE WE CAN TEST THE LORD

Why do you think it is important not to put the Lord to the test, aside from giving and receiving?

SATAN'S ARSENAL

The devil's temptations will always be with natural things, such as hunger, identity, authority, and power. He looks for weaknesses, just like he saw that Jesus was hungry. We know that Jesus was tempted but never sinned; this means that we can resist temptation without sinning. Let's follow Jesus' example when the devil attacks.

THE FOCAL POINT

According to Luke 10:19, demons are referred to as snakes and scorpions. We have more authority because of our physical bodies and being filled with the Holy Spirit than any demonic entity. In what ways has Jesus positioned His body, the Church, to take the world back from the enemy?

THE NATURAL WORLD WAS NOT MADE FOR SPIRITS

What is the difference between humans and spirits that allows only people to be saved, not the devil and angels? Why is this a vital understanding when confronted with the false doctrine that they can be saved?

THE ULTIMATE ACT OF SPIRITUAL WARFARE

FOCUS POINT

The most powerful act of spiritual warfare is to lead someone to Jesus Christ, helping them transition from darkness into light. Use this time to create a prayer list of those you believe need salvation. Seek guidance from the Lord on how He can use you to minister to them. Then, write a prayer for them.

JESUS INTERCEDES FOR US

We know that Jesus intercedes for us. In John 17, Jesus prays for His disciples and for all those who will become believers. Read John 17. What part of His prayer spoke to you the most and why?

THE DEVIL EATS DIRT

The opposite of ministering to someone is accusing them. When love is present, people will want to see God do something in another person's life. However, when love is absent, accusations and offenses become easier targets in someone's life. If there is someone in your life with whom you are offended, take this time to repent and release that person.

DON'T SURRENDER TO HIS VOICE!

What are some practical ways to remain "sober-minded" with the Word of God to avoid the influence of negative thoughts and the devouring effects of the devil?

THE SHIELD OF FAITH

How can taking control of your thoughts and utilizing the shield of faith transform your approach to spiritual warfare and enhance your overall sense of peace and purpose?

BECOME RE-SENSITIZED TO THE HOLY SPIRIT

Consider these thoughts: "Five minutes in the presence of God can do more than five years of therapy," and "Presence-based living creates power-based children." What do these mean to you?

RETURN TO THE FOUNDATION

PERSONAL REFLECTIONS

A culture must remember the faithful leaders—those who dedicated their lives to laying a foundation for future generations to know God and fulfill their God-given calling. In every person's salvation story, there is typically someone who invested in them and shared the gospel, and sometimes it may be more than one person. Take a moment to reflect on who played a role in helping you find Jesus. Perhaps it was a praying grandmother or a friend who invited you to church. There is a significant individual that the Lord used to bring you into His family. Write about how this person made a meaningful impact on your life.

CHAPTER EIGHT

UNLOCK THE SPIRITUAL REALM

SCRIPTURES

1. **Hebrews 11:1**—Now faith is the substance of things hoped for, the evidence of things not seen.

2. **Romans 1:20**—For since the creation of the world His invisible attributes are clearly seen, being understood by the things that are made, even His eternal power and Godhead, so that they are without excuse.

3. **First Corinthians 15:46**—However, the spiritual is not first, but the natural, and afterward the spiritual.

4. **Hebrews 7:8**—Here mortal men receive tithes, but there he receives them, of whom it is witnessed that he lives.

5. **John 1:14**—And the Word became flesh and dwelt among us, and we beheld His glory, the glory as of the only begotten of the Father, full of grace and truth.

6. **Romans 8:5-14**—For those who live according to the flesh set their minds on the things of the flesh, but those who live according to the Spirit, the things of the Spirit. [6] For to be carnally minded is death, but to be spiritually minded is life and peace.[7] Because the carnal mind is enmity against God; for it is not subject to the law of God, nor indeed can be.[8] So then, those who are in the flesh cannot please God. [9] But you are not in the flesh but in the Spirit, if indeed the Spirit of God dwells in you. Now if anyone does not have the Spirit of Christ, he is not His. [10] And if Christ is in you, the body is dead because of sin, but the Spirit is life because of righteousness. [11] But if the Spirit of Him who raised Jesus from the dead dwells

in you, He who raised Christ from the dead will also give life to your mortal bodies through His Spirit who dwells in you. [12] Therefore, brethren, we are debtors—not to the flesh, to live according to the flesh. [13] For if you live according to the flesh you will die; but if by the Spirit you put to death the deeds of the body, you will live. [14] For as many as are led by the Spirit of God, these are sons of God.

7. **Romans 7:22-23**—For I delight in the law of God according to the inward man. [23] But I see another law in my members, warring against ***the law of my mind***, and bringing me into captivity to the law of sin which is in my members.

8. **Matthew 6:33**—But seek first the kingdom of God and His righteousness, and all these things shall be added to you.

9. **Romans 12:2**—And do not be conformed to this world, but be transformed by the **renewing of your mind**, that you may prove what is that good and acceptable and perfect will of God.

10. **Ephesians 2:8-9**—For by grace you have been saved through faith, and that not of yourselves; it is the gift of God, [9] not of works, lest anyone should boast.

11. **Matthew 4:4-7**—But He answered and said, "It is written, 'Man shall not live by bread alone, but by every word that proceeds from the mouth of God.' " [5] Then the devil took Him up into the holy city, set Him on the pinnacle of the temple, [6] and said to Him, "If You are the Son of God, throw Yourself down. For it is written: 'He shall give His angels charge over you,' and, 'In their hands they shall bear you up, lest you dash your foot against a stone.' " [7] Jesus said to him, "It is written again, 'You shall not tempt the Lord your God.' "

12. **Luke 4:4-10**—But Jesus answered him, saying, "It is written, 'Man shall not live by bread alone, but by every word of God.' " [5] Then the devil, taking Him up on a high mountain, showed Him all the kingdoms of the world in a moment of time. [6] And the devil said to Him, "All this authority I will give You, and their glory; for this has been delivered to me, and I give it to whomever I wish. [7] Therefore, if You will worship before me, all will be Yours." [8] And Jesus answered and said to him, "Get behind Me, Satan! For it is written, 'You shall worship the Lord your God, and Him only you shall serve.' " [9] Then he brought Him to Jerusalem, set Him on the pinnacle of the temple, and said to Him, "If You are the Son of God, throw Yourself down from here. [10] For it is written: 'He shall give His angels charge over you, to keep you.' "

13. **Matthew 24:4, 8-13**—And Jesus answered and said to them: "Take heed that no one deceives you... [8] All these are the beginning of sorrows. [9] Then they will deliver you up to tribulation and kill you, and you will be hated by all nations for My name's sake. [10] And then many will be offended, will betray one another, and will hate one another. [11] Then many false prophets will rise up and deceive many. [12] And because lawlessness will abound, the love of many will grow cold. [13] But he who endures to the end shall be saved."

14. **First Peter 5:8 NIV**—Be alert and of sober mind. Your enemy the devil prowls around like a roaring lion looking for someone to devour.

15. **James 4:7 NIV**—Submit yourselves, then, to God. Resist the devil, and he will flee from you.

16. **Hebrews 5:14**—But solid food belongs to those who are of full age, that is, those who by reason of use have their senses exercised to discern both good and evil.

17. **Second Peter 1:3-4 NIV**—His divine power has given us everything we need for a godly life through our knowledge of him who called us by his own glory and goodness. [4] Through these he has given us his very great and precious promises, so that through them you may participate in the divine nature, having escaped the corruption in the world caused by evil desires.

18. **Luke 10:17-20**—Then the seventy returned with joy, saying, "Lord, even the demons are subject to us in Your name." [18] And He said to them, "I saw Satan fall like lightning from heaven. [19] Behold, I give you authority to trample on serpents and scorpions, and over all the power of the enemy, and nothing shall by any means hurt you. [20] Nevertheless do not rejoice in this, that the spirits are subject to you, but rather rejoice because your names are written in heaven."

19. **First John 5:4-5 NIV**—For everyone born of God overcomes the world. This is the victory that has overcome the world, even our faith. [5] Who is it that overcomes the world? Only the one who believes that Jesus is the Son of God.

The concept that the natural comes before the spiritual is essential for effectiveness in the Kingdom of God. What are your thoughts on the idea of the natural preceding the spiritual?

___

___

THE NATURAL (HERE) THE SPIRIT (THERE)

Explain the difference between the natural (here) and the spiritual (there), and why the natural comes first?

IF YOU WORK THE WORD, THE WORD WORKS

According to Romans 8:5, when someone lives according to the flesh, their mindset is focused on the flesh. This understanding can be observed through their actions and attitudes, which often reflect worldly desires. It's evident when someone's thoughts and behaviors prioritize immediate gratification over spiritual growth. How can we encourage others to shift their focus from the flesh to a more spiritually oriented mindset?

THE LAW OF THE MIND

Have you ever meditated on the promises in Scripture until you saw the fulfillment of that promise come to pass? If you have experienced this in your life, describe the situation and what you learned through the process. If you have not experienced this, what scriptures would you meditate on to see the promises of God come to fruition in your life?

THE NATURAL COMES FIRST

In context, 1 Corinthians 15:46 references Adam as the natural and Jesus as the spiritual. Read 1 Corinthians 15:44-49 and write how this conclusion was made.

GETTING A SUPERNATURAL REACTION

A faith action is the first step toward receiving a supernatural manifestation. What are some examples of faith actions you have taken that resulted in supernatural outcomes?

THE SPIRIT REALM IS THE PARENT FORCE

How does the process of sowing and reaping apply to the natural and spiritual?

GRACE AND FAITH

FOCUS POINT

Reading and memorizing the Bible alone is not sufficient to overcome a carnal and unrenewed mind. There is a process that involves reading, memorizing, and then truly believing the Word. Refer to Joshua 1:8 for guidance on how to become prosperous and successful. Remember that prosperity and success extend beyond financial matters; they can apply to all areas of your life.

To deepen your understanding, take the following steps:

1. Read Joshua 1:8: Spend some time with this verse and reflect on its meaning.
2. Write it down: Take a moment to write Joshua 1:8 in your own words. This will help you internalize its message.
3. Pray for understanding: If you find the concept of Joshua 1:8 challenging, take time to pray. Ask the Holy Spirit to minister to you with the truth of His Word.

By engaging in this process, you are exercising faith in God's written Word in all areas of your life and developing a renewed mind.

A WORD OF CAUTION

Why are the teachings that say "God's grace will cover everything," or "You don't need the Word," considered harmful to believers?

THE DOMINO EFFECT

In the example of the domino effect, we can see how negative influences from others can impact our attitude and day. Have you ever experienced a situation like this? How did you respond, whether positively or negatively, and what did you learn from that experience?

REJOICE THAT YOUR NAME IS WRITTEN IN HEAVEN

PERSONAL REFLECTIONS

When the disciples returned to Jesus after being sent out in pairs, they were filled with excitement because they were able to cast out demons. Interestingly, Jesus didn't focus on their enthusiasm. Instead, He told them to rejoice because their names were written in heaven. Often, people pay more attention to the things of the devil and his evil forces. While it's thrilling that demons submit to the name of Jesus, we should be even more thankful that our names are recorded in heaven.

During this time of personal reflection, take a moment to thank the Lord for your salvation and for the many blessings He has bestowed upon you. Write 1 John 5:4-5 in your own words, transforming it into a form of prayer and declaration.

CHAPTER NINE

WEAPONS OF WAR

SCRIPTURES

1. **Second Corinthians 10:3-6**—For though we walk in the flesh, we do not war according to the flesh. [4] For the weapons of our warfare are not carnal but mighty in God for pulling down strongholds, [5] casting down arguments and every high thing that exalts itself against the knowledge of God, bringing every thought into captivity to the obedience of Christ, [6] and being ready to punish all disobedience when your obedience is fulfilled.

2. **First Peter 1:13**—Therefore gird up the loins of your mind, be sober, and rest your hope fully upon the grace that is to be brought to you at the revelation of Jesus Christ.

3. **Romans 12:3**—For I say, through the grace given to me, to everyone who is among you, not to think of himself more highly than he ought to think, but to think soberly, as God has dealt to each one a measure of faith.

4. **First Samuel 16:23**—And so it was, whenever the spirit from God was upon Saul, that David would take a harp and play it with his hand. Then Saul would become refreshed and well, and the distressing spirit would depart from him.

5. **Second Kings 3:15-16**—"But now bring me a musician." Then it happened, when the musician played, that the hand of the Lord came upon him. [16] And he said, "Thus says the Lord: 'Make this valley full of ditches.'"

6. **Luke 10:20**—Nevertheless do not rejoice in this, that the spirits are subject to you, but rather rejoice because your names are written in heaven.

7. **Ephesians 6:10-13**—Finally, my brethren, be strong in the Lord and in the power of His might. [11] Put on the whole armor of God, that you may be able to stand against the wiles of the devil. [12] For we do not wrestle against flesh and blood, but against principalities, against powers, against the rulers of the darkness of this age, against spiritual hosts of wickedness in the heavenly places. [13] Therefore take up the whole armor of God, that you may be able to withstand in the evil day, and having done all, to stand.

8. **Psalm 91:3**—Surely He shall deliver you from the snare of the fowler and from the perilous pestilence.

9. **Ephesians 6:14-18 NIV**—Stand firm then, with the belt of truth buckled around your waist, with the breastplate of righteousness in place, [15] and with your feet fitted with the readiness that comes from the gospel of peace. [16] In addition to all this, take up the shield of faith, with which you can extinguish all the flaming arrows of the evil one. [17] Take the helmet of salvation and the sword of the Spirit, which is the word of God. [18] And pray in the Spirit on all occasions with all kinds of prayers and requests. With this in mind, be alert and always keep on praying for all the Lord's people.

10. **John 17:17**—Sanctify them by Your truth. Your word is truth.

11. **Luke 2:52**—And Jesus increased in wisdom and stature, and in favor with God and men.

12. **Hebrews 4:12**—For the Word of God is living and powerful, and sharper than any two-edged sword, piercing even to the division of soul and spirit, and of joints and marrow, and is a discerner of the thoughts and intents of the heart.

13. **Matthew 4:4-11**—But He answered and said, "It is written, 'Man shall not live by bread alone, but by every word that proceeds from the mouth of God.'" [5] Then the devil took Him up into the holy city, set Him on the pinnacle of the temple, [6] and said to Him, "If You are the Son of God, throw Yourself down. For it is written: 'He shall give His angels charge over you,' and, 'In their hands they shall bear you up, Lest you dash your foot against a stone.'" [7] Jesus said to him, "It is written again, 'You shall not tempt the Lord your God.'" [8] Again, the devil took Him up on an exceedingly high mountain, and showed Him all the kingdoms of the world and their glory. [9] And he said to Him, "All these things I will give You if You will fall

down and worship me." [10] Then Jesus said to him, "Away with you, Satan! For it is written, 'You shall worship the Lord your God, and Him only you shall serve.'" [11] Then the devil left Him, and behold, angels came and ministered to Him.

14. **Luke 4:3-12**—And the devil said to Him, "If You are the Son of God, command this stone to become bread." [4] But Jesus answered him, saying, "It is written, 'Man shall not live by bread alone, but by every word of God.'" [5] Then the devil, taking Him up on a high mountain, showed Him all the kingdoms of the world in a moment of time. [6] And the devil said to Him, "All this authority I will give You, and their glory; for this has been delivered to me, and I give it to whomever I wish. [7] Therefore, if You will worship before me, all will be Yours." [8] And Jesus answered and said to him, "Get behind Me, Satan! For it is written, 'You shall worship the Lord your God, and Him only you shall serve.'" [9] Then he brought Him to Jerusalem, set Him on the pinnacle of the temple, and said to Him, "If You are the Son of God, throw Yourself down from here. [10] For it is written: 'He shall give His angels charge over you, to keep you,' [11] and, 'In their hands they shall bear you up, lest you dash your foot against a stone.'" [12] And Jesus answered and said to him, "It has been said, 'You shall not tempt the LORD your God.'"

15. **Second Peter 1:2-4 NLT**—May God give you more and more grace and peace as you grow in your knowledge of God and Jesus our Lord. [3] By his divine power, God has given us everything we need for living a godly life. We have received all of this by coming to know him, the one who called us to himself by means of his marvelous glory and excellence. [4] And because of his glory and excellence, he has given us great and precious promises. These are the promises that enable you to share his divine nature and escape the world's corruption caused by human desires.

Luke 6:45 says, "A good man out of the good treasure of his heart brings forth good; and an evil man out of the evil treasure of his heart brings forth evil. For out of the abundance of the heart his mouth speaks." How does this scripture show us that disobedience is a reflection of the heart and mind?

____

____

____

____

SOBER-MINDED EFFECTIVENESS

There are three significant actions that believers are called to do in 1 Peter 1:13. For each point, write a brief statement of what that looks like in your life.

1. Gird up the loins of your mind.

2. Be sober.

3. Rest your hope fully upon grace that is to be brought to you at the revelation of Jesus Christ.

PEACE REPELLED SAUL'S DEMON

FOCUS POINT

Overcoming the devil's powers begins with shifting our focus away from ourselves and directing it toward the Lord. Praise and worship are essential tools for this. When we worship wholeheartedly, the enemy's tactics and weapons lose their impact, and we are filled with the power to overcome. Take a moment to play some worship music and spend time with Jesus. Invite His Holy Spirit to surround you and guide you in any situation you need to overcome. Consider writing down your prayer and noting anything you hear Him speak to you.

MUSIC BROUGHT PEACE TO ELISHA

The devil brings turmoil, fear, and uncertainty. Thankfully, God brings peace. Peace that surpasses understanding. Read Philippians 4:6-7. Write it down and memorize it, knowing that God provides us with peace to hear His Voice over the enemies.

YOU STILL NEED JESUS!

Many believers are walking around not knowing what they have through Jesus. They don't understand the authority they have. Because of this, the devil is influencing the masses even in the Church. How can God use you to bring clarity and light to those who are struggling with this understanding?

FULL METAL SOLDIER

The devil uses the process of persuasion to convince people to believe him instead of God, similar to how he persuaded Eve to eat the forbidden fruit in the Garden of Eden (*see* Genesis 3:1-6). How is this possible? According to the Greek word *kakodaímon*, he acts as an evil genius. An "evil genius" is defined as a person who exerts a strong, negative influence over others. While the devil influences the masses, we are called to be a light to those around us. Let's strive to be a light and help others come to an understanding of who Jesus is!

TAKE UP THE WHOLE ARMOR AND STAND IN VICTORY

According to the examples given, what "stand" does not mean, have there been times when these thoughts attempted to enter your mind? If so, what was your process of removing them? If not, what has been the main reason you have been able to resist these types of thoughts?

____

____

____

____

____

____

____

____

____

THE FULL ARMOR OF GOD

PERSONAL REFLECTIONS

For this Personal Reflections moment, read the remainder of Chapter Nine in the main book. For each section, describe what each piece of armor signifies to you and how you are incorporating it into your daily life.

BELT OF TRUTH

____

____

BREASTPLATE OF RIGHTEOUSNESS

FEET FITTED FOR THE GOSPEL

SHIELD OF FAITH

HELMET OF SALVATION

SWORD OF THE SPIRIT

SECTION THREE

New Covenant Horsepower

CHAPTER TEN

Preservation of Jesus' Bloodline

SCRIPTURES

1. **Jude 1:5**—But I want to remind you, though you once knew this, that the Lord, having saved the people out of the land of Egypt, afterward destroyed those who did not believe.

2. **Jude 1:6**—And the angels who did not keep their proper domain, but left their own abode, He has reserved everlasting chains under darkness for the judgment of the great day.

3. **Jude 1:7**—As Sodom and Gomorrah, and the cities around them in a similar manner to these, having given themselves over to sexual immorality and gone after **strange flesh,** are set forth as an example, suffering the vengeance of eternal fire.

4. **Genesis 19:1-5**—Now the two angels came to Sodom in the evening, and Lot was sitting in the gate of Sodom. When Lot saw them, he rose to meet them, and he bowed himself with his face toward the ground. [2] And he said, "Here now, my lords, please turn in to your servant's house and spend the night, and wash your feet; then you may rise early and go on your way." And they said, "No, but we will spend the night in the open square." [3] But he insisted strongly; so they turned in to him and entered his house. Then he made them a feast, and baked unleavened bread, and they ate. [4] Now before they lay down, the men of the city, the men of Sodom, both old and young, all the people from every quarter, surrounded the house. [5] And they called to Lot and said to him, "Where are the men who came to you tonight? Bring them out to us that we may know them carnally."

5. **Genesis 3:15**—And I will put enmity between you and the woman, and between your seed and her Seed; He shall bruise your head, and you shall bruise His heel.

6. **Jude 1:8**—Likewise also these dreamers defile the flesh, reject authority, and speak evil of dignitaries.

7. **Jude 1:9-13**—Yet Michael the archangel, in contending with the devil, when he disputed about the body of Moses, dared not bring against him a reviling accusation, but said, "The Lord rebuke you!" [10] But these speak evil of whatever they do not know; and whatever they know naturally, like brute beasts, in these things they corrupt themselves. [11] Woe to them! For they have gone in the way of Cain, have run greedily in the error of Balaam for profit, and perished in the rebellion of Korah. [12] These are spots in your love feasts, while they feast with you without fear, serving only themselves. They are clouds without water, carried about by the winds; late autumn trees without fruit, twice dead, pulled up by the roots; [13] raging waves of the sea, foaming up their own shame; ***wandering stars*** for whom is reserved the blackness of darkness forever.

8. **Jude 1:14-15**—Now Enoch, the seventh from Adam, prophesied about these men also, saying, "Behold, the Lord comes with ten thousands of His saints, [15] to execute judgment on all, to convict all who are ungodly among them of all their ungodly deeds which they have committed in an ungodly way, and of all the harsh things which ungodly sinners have spoken against Him."

9. **Jude 1:16-18**—These are grumblers, complainers, walking according to their own lusts; and they mouth great swelling words, flattering people to gain advantage. [17] But you, beloved, remember the words which were spoken before by the apostles of our Lord Jesus Christ: [18] how they told you that there would be mockers in the last time who would walk according to their own ungodly lusts.

10. **Jude 1:19**—These are sensual persons, who cause divisions, not having the Spirit.

11. **Hebrews 5:14**—But solid food belongs to those who are of full age, that is, those who by reason of use have their senses exercised to discern both good and evil.

12. **Galatians 5:22-23**—But the fruit of the Spirit is love, joy, peace, longsuffering, kindness, goodness, faithfulness, [23] gentleness, self-control. Against such there is no law.

13. **Genesis 6:1-2**—Now it came to pass, when men began to multiply on the face of the earth, and daughters were born to them, [2] that ***the sons of God*** saw the daughters of men, that they were beautiful; and they took wives for themselves of all whom they chose.

14. **Genesis 6:3**—And the Lord said, "My Spirit shall not strive with man forever, for he is indeed flesh; yet his days shall be one hundred and twenty years."

15. **Genesis 6:4**—There were ***giants*** on the earth ***in those days, and also afterward***, when the sons of God came in to the daughters of men and they bore children to them. Those were the mighty men who were of old, men of renown.

16. **Numbers 13:33**—There we saw the giants (the descendants of Anak came from the giants); and we were like grasshoppers in our own sight, and so we were in their sight.

17. **Genesis 6:8-9**—But Noah found grace in the eyes of the Lord. [9] This is the genealogy of Noah. Noah was a just man, ***perfect in his generations.*** Noah walked with God.

Often, people struggle to "see" Jesus because they are consumed by selfishness. This self-centeredness becomes a distraction and can prevent them from recognizing all that Jesus has to offer. With this understanding, how does one begin to lose a spiritual battle?

___

___

___

___

___

___

___

___

___

___

___

WISDOM FROM JUDE

God desires to be believed and trusted. Doubt can lead to fear and misguide people toward a path of destruction. Just as the Israelites chose fear over God's promises, how do you see people making similar choices in the world today?

According to Jude 1:18, there will be mockers in the last days who follow their ungodly desires. In today's society, we observe people mocking the Word and belittling believers. These individuals treat spiritual matters as a joke and encourage others to join in their mischievous behavior. Based on Hebrews 5:14, what are these individuals failing to do, and how are they not applying this verse in their lives?

THE PLAN TO POLLUTE JESUS' BLOODLINE

FOCUS POINT

According to Genesis 3:15, God established a plan of redemption for humanity. We understand that Jesus is the divine seed whom the devil and the fallen angels tried to prevent from entering the world. Thankfully, their plans failed, and the greatest gift to humanity was born. Jesus came in the flesh to set the captives free, empower the saints with the tools to overcome the enemy, and provide the promise of eternity in heaven. Everything God has done throughout history has been motivated by love. For more insight, read 2 Peter 3:9 and reflect on why God acts out of love.

BLOODLINE PRESERVATION THROUGH NOAH

How does the understanding that angels abandoned their God-assigned roles and procreated with women, resulting in the creation of "strange flesh," help explain why God needed to send the flood to preserve Noah, his family, and the future of humanity?

PERSONAL REFLECTIONS

In this chapter, we explored how the fallen angels chose rebellion over obedience. Alongside the devil, they attempted to corrupt the lineage intended for the coming Messiah. As a result of these actions, God intervened with a plan for redemption. Although this plan may have seemed harsh to some, it was ultimately an expression of God's grace, designed to save future generations.

Now, consider Luke 2:8-14. What distinguishes the angels mentioned in Luke from the rebellious angels of the Old Testament? Why do you think these angels were rejoicing at the sight of the baby wrapped in swaddling clothes?

CHAPTER ELEVEN

JESUS CHANGES EVERYTHING

SCRIPTURES

1. **Jude 1:6 NLT**—And I remind you of the angels who did not stay within the limits of authority God gave them but left the place where they belonged. God has kept them securely chained in prisons of darkness, waiting for the great day of judgment.

2. **Revelation 9:13-16**—Then the sixth angel sounded: And I heard a voice from the four horns of the golden altar which is before God, [14] saying to the sixth angel who had the trumpet, "Release the four angels who are bound at the great river Euphrates." [15] So the four angels, who had been prepared for the hour and day and month and year, were released to kill a third of mankind. [16] Now the number of the army of the horsemen was two hundred million; I heard the number of them.

3. **Daniel 10:13**—But the prince of the kingdom of Persia withstood me twenty-one days; and behold, Michael, one of the chief princes, came to help me, for I had been left alone there with the kings of Persia.

4. **John 12:31**—Now is the judgment of this world; now the ruler of this world will be cast out.

5. **Matthew 12:43**—When an unclean spirit goes out of a man, he goes through dry places, seeking rest, and finds none.

6. **Luke 22:3**—Then Satan entered Judas, surnamed Iscariot, who was numbered among the twelve.

7. **John 13:27**—Now after the piece of bread, Satan entered him. Then Jesus said to him, "What you do, do quickly."

8. **Mark 9:25 KJV**—When Jesus saw that the people came running together, he rebuked the foul spirit, saying unto him, Thou dumb and deaf spirit, I charge thee, come out of him, and enter no more into him.

9. **Matthew 8:26**—But He said to them, "Why are you fearful, O you of little faith?" Then He arose and rebuked the winds and the sea, and there was a great calm.

10. **Mark 4:37-40**—And a great windstorm arose, and the waves beat into the boat, so that it was already filling. [38] But He was in the stern, asleep on a pillow. And they awoke Him and said to Him, "Teacher, do You not care that we are perishing?" [39] Then He arose and rebuked the wind, and said to the sea, "Peace, be still!" And the wind ceased and there was a great calm. [40] But He said to them, "Why are you so fearful? How is it that you have no faith?"

11. **Isaiah 14:16**—Those who see you will gaze at you, and consider you, saying: "Is this the man who made the earth tremble, who shook kingdoms?"

12. **Second Corinthians 4:1-6**—Therefore, since we have this ministry, as we have received mercy, we do not lose heart. [2] But we have renounced the hidden things of shame, not walking in craftiness nor handling the word of God deceitfully, but by manifestation of the truth commending ourselves to every man's conscience in the sight of God. [3] But even if our gospel is veiled, it is veiled to those who are perishing, [4] whose minds the god of this age has blinded, who do not believe, lest the light of the gospel of the glory of Christ, who is the image of God, should shine on them. [5] For we do not preach ourselves, but Christ Jesus the Lord, and ourselves your bondservants for Jesus' sake. [6] For it is the God who commanded light to shine out of darkness, who has shone in our hearts to give the light of the knowledge of the glory of God in the face of Jesus Christ.

13. **Second Corinthians 12:7**—And lest I should be exalted above measure by the abundance of the revelations, a thorn in the flesh was given to me, a messenger of Satan to buffet me, lest I be exalted above measure.

14. **Acts 26:16**—But rise and stand on your feet; for I have appeared to you for this purpose, to make you a minister and a witness both of the things which you have seen and of the things which I will yet reveal to you.

15. **Matthew 9:35-36**—Then Jesus went about all the cities and villages, teaching in their synagogues, preaching the gospel of the kingdom, and healing every sickness

and every disease among the people. [36] But when He saw the multitudes, He was moved with compassion for them, because they were weary and scattered, like sheep having no shepherd.

16. **Matthew 9:37-38**—Then He said to His disciples, "The harvest truly is plentiful, but the laborers are few. [38] Therefore pray the Lord of the harvest to send out laborers into His harvest."

17. **Romans 10:14**—How then shall they call on Him in whom they have not believed? And how shall they believe in Him of whom they have not heard? And how shall they hear without a preacher?

18. **Acts 9:3**—As he journeyed he came near Damascus, and suddenly a light shone around him from heaven.

19. **Acts 9:10-19**—Now there was a certain disciple at Damascus named Ananias; and to him the Lord said in a vision, "Ananias." And he said, "Here I am, Lord." [11] So the Lord said to him, "Arise and go to the street called Straight, and inquire at the house of Judas for one called Saul of Tarsus, for behold, he is praying. [12] And in a vision he has seen a man named Ananias coming in and putting his hand on him, so that he might receive his sight." [13] Then Ananias answered, "Lord, I have heard from many about this man, how much harm he has done to Your saints in Jerusalem. [14] And here he has authority from the chief priests to bind all who call on Your name." [15] But the Lord said to him, "Go, for he is a chosen vessel of Mine to bear My name before Gentiles, kings, and the children of Israel. [16] For I will show him how many things he must suffer for My name's sake." [17] And Ananias went his way and entered the house; and laying his hands on him he said, "Brother Saul, the Lord Jesus, who appeared to you on the road as you came, has sent me that you may receive your sight and be filled with the Holy Spirit." [18] Immediately there fell from his eyes something like scales, and he received his sight at once; and he arose and was baptized. [19] So when he had received food, he was strengthened. Then Saul spent some days with the disciples at Damascus.

20. **Matthew 9:38**—Therefore pray the Lord of the harvest to send out laborers into His harvest.

21. **Luke 10:2**—Then He said to them, "The harvest truly is great, but the laborers are few; therefore pray the Lord of the harvest to send out laborers into His harvest."

22. **Revelation 12:10-11**—Then I heard a loud voice saying in heaven, "Now salvation, and strength, and the kingdom of our God, and the power of His Christ have come, for the accuser of our brethren, who accused them before our God day and night, has been cast down. [11] And they overcame him by the blood of the Lamb and by the word of their testimony, and they did not love their lives to the death."

23. **John 10:10**—The thief does not come except to steal, and to kill, and to destroy. I have come that they may have life, and that they may have it more abundantly.

24. **Jude 1:20**—But you, beloved, building yourselves up on your most holy faith, praying in the Holy Spirit.

25. **Revelation 12:11**—And they overcame him by the blood of the Lamb and by the word of their testimony, and they did not love their lives to the death.

ANGELS, FALLEN ANGELS, AND DEMONS

From your understanding, is there a difference between fallen angels and demons? If so, what are the main differences you see between them?

OUR WAR IS AGAINST DISEMBODIED, FOUL, AND EVIL SPIRITS

Matthew 12:43 states that demons seek rest after being cast out of a person. Understanding that they require a human body to operate, how do you think they find rest when they discover a willing vessel?

OLD TESTAMENT INTERACTION WITH DEMONS

When David played the harp for Saul, the demons became silent. When Jesus arrived, those demons had to leave their host's body and could not remain. Understanding this—witnessing how the devil has tormented God's creation throughout history—and then seeing Jesus come to put an end to that, can lead us to ponder how God and Jesus felt the first time He cast out a demon. That's a profound thought.

ANGELS AND POSSESSION

Based on what you know about angels and demons, write a few differences between the two.

"REBUKE" IS NOT A MAGIC WORD

Jesus rebuking the demonic spirit in a young boy or a storm wasn't what changed the scenario. What was it exactly that set the boy free and stripped the storm of its power?

USING THE WORD "REBUKE" IN SPIRITUAL WARFARE

In Mark 4:37-40, Jesus rebukes a storm that frightened His disciples. In verse 39, He commands, "Peace, be still!" This illustrates the significance of knowing that peace can calm any storm in our lives. Take a moment to look up the definition of *peace* and write it down. Remember to thank God for the gift of peace!

THE "REAL" KINGDOM OF DARKNESS

An important revelation is on the way—a day when the true nature of the devil will be exposed. Many people will be surprised to learn that he is not who they thought he was. Currently, some are deceived into thinking that the devil is good, as he often presents himself as an angel of light (*see* 2 Corinthians 11:14). Understanding his true identity will empower believers and help them avoid falling into fear.

PERSECUTION FOR THE WORD'S SAKE

What was the "thorn in the flesh" that Paul was experiencing?

PREACH THE GOSPEL FOR THE WIN!

FOCUS POINT

According to Wikipedia, about 150,000 people die every day worldwide.[1] As of this writing in 2025, the Christian population in the world is 28.8 percent. This percentage has decreased by 1.8 percent over the past ten years.[2] Jesus is the only way to heaven. Given that 150,000 people die each day, this means that only about 43,200 people will be going to heaven. On average, this leaves 106,800 people who will not. This sobering statistic should concern every believer.

Just as compassion led Jesus to heal the sick, cast out demons, and minister to others, these numbers should inspire us to take action. Matthew 9:37-38 reminds us that the harvest is ready. Take this time to pray for those who are lost. Ask the Lord who you can minister to today—it could be a coworker, a friend, or a family member. If someone comes to mind, be obedient and reach out to them. You never know what the outcome will be until you take that first step. Remember that 2 Corinthians 6:2 (NLT) says, "Today is the day for salvation." Let this be your declaration to all who need to hear the gospel.

USING PRAYER IN SPIRITUAL WARFARE

Unfortunately, we live in a time when many people in the United States have never heard about Jesus and what He has done for them. This situation may seem unimaginable, but the current generation of newborns is growing up in families where there are no praying grandparents. Many grandparents, who were among the first to identify as atheists, raised their children in their belief. As a result, their children were not taught about Jesus as the way to eternal life. In turn, the third generation has not heard the good news of the gospel.

There is strength in having praying grandparents and parents, but sadly, many do not have that support. We pray for God to send workers to minister to those who lack this coverage in their lives, so they may have a transformative encounter with God that changes their lives and impacts future generations.

PRAY THE LORD OF THE HARVEST

Have you tried to minister to someone in your life, but they haven't listened to what you have to say? This is quite common, especially when the person is familiar to you. Sometimes it takes someone outside their usual circle to share the truth for them to be receptive. Take a moment to write down their names and pray for God to send the right person to reach out to them. Additionally, pray that they are open to hearing what the Spirit is conveying through that individual.

THE LANDING PAD

How do you think the demons know if you believe in the authority given by Jesus?

GOING RED IN THE BLOOD OF THE LAMB

PERSONAL REFLECTIONS

As a believer, you are empowered to overcome everything the enemy throws at you. Even if he tries to steal, kill, and destroy, we know that the devil cannot win because you have the authority through the blood of Jesus and your testimony. You are destined for victory, so remember—the battle is not over until you win!

Take this time to seek the Lord and spend time praying in the Holy Spirit. If you have not yet been filled with the Holy Spirit and do not have the evidence of speaking in tongues, now is the time to ask the Lord to fill you, just as He did in the book of Acts. You need to exercise your faith and take action by moving your tongue; He won't do it for you.

You can also reach out to our prayer team, and they will be happy to pray for you to be filled with the Holy Spirit. For our contact information, please visit JosephZ.com.

CHAPTER TWELVE

THE GREAT COMMISSION

SCRIPTURES

1. **Mark 16:14-18**—Later He appeared to the eleven as they sat at the table; and He rebuked their unbelief and hardness of heart, because they did not believe those who had seen Him after He had risen. [15] And He said to them, "Go into all the world and preach the gospel to every creature. [16] He who believes and is baptized will be saved; but he who does not believe will be condemned. [17] And these signs will follow those who believe: In My name they will cast out demons; they will speak with new tongues; [18] they will take up serpents; and if they drink anything deadly, it will by no means hurt them; they will lay hands on the sick, and they will recover."

2. **John 4:24**—God is Spirit, and those who worship Him must worship in spirit and truth.

3. **John 6:63**—It is the Spirit who gives life; the flesh profits nothing. The words that I speak to you are spirit, and they are life.

4. **Galatians 5:16**—I say then: Walk in the Spirit, and you shall not fulfill the lust of the flesh.

5. **Acts 28:1-10**—Now when they had escaped, they then found out that the island was called Malta. [2] And the natives showed us unusual kindness; for they kindled a fire and made us all welcome, because of the rain that was falling and because of the cold. [3] But when Paul had gathered a bundle of sticks and laid them on the fire, a viper came out because of the heat, and fastened on his hand. [4] So when the natives saw the creature hanging from his hand, they said to one another, "No doubt this man is a murderer, whom, though he has escaped the sea, yet justice does not allow

to live." [5] But he shook off the creature into the fire and suffered no harm. [6] However, they were expecting that he would swell up or suddenly fall down dead. But after they had looked for a long time and saw no harm come to him, they changed their minds and said that he was a god. [7] In that region there was an estate of the leading citizen of the island, whose name was Publius, who received us and entertained us courteously for three days. [8] And it happened that the father of Publius lay sick of a fever and dysentery. Paul went in to him and prayed, and he laid his hands on him and healed him. [9] So when this was done, the rest of those on the island who had diseases also came and were healed. [10] They also honored us in many ways; and when we departed, they provided such things as were necessary.

6. **First John 3:8**—He who sins is of the devil, for the devil has sinned from the beginning. For this purpose the Son of God was manifested, that He might destroy the works of the devil.

7. **First John 4:17**—Love has been perfected among us in this: that we may have boldness in the day of judgment; because as He is, so are we in this world.

8. **Revelation 20:11**—Then I saw a great white throne and Him who sat on it, from whose face the earth and the heaven fled away. And there was found no place for them.

9. **Revelation 21:1**—Now I saw a new heaven and a new earth, for the first heaven and the first earth had passed away. Also there was no more sea.

10. **Matthew 25:41**—Then He will also say to those on the left hand, "Depart from Me, you cursed, into the everlasting fire prepared for the devil and his angels."

11. **Revelation 20:14**—Then Death and Hades were cast into the lake of fire. This is the second death.

12. **First Corinthians 15:40**—There are also celestial bodies and terrestrial bodies; but the glory of the celestial is one, and the glory of the terrestrial is another.

13. **Second Corinthians 5:8**—We are confident, yes, well pleased rather to be absent from the body and to be present with the Lord.

14. **Romans 8:29**—For whom He foreknew, He also predestined to be conformed to the image of His Son, that He might be the firstborn among many brethren.

15. **Revelation 19:16**—And He has on His robe and on His thigh a name written: KING OF KINGS AND LORD OF LORDS.

16. **Joshua 23:10**—One man of you shall chase a thousand, for the Lord your God is He who fights for you, as He promised you.

17. **Isaiah 53:1**—Who has believed our report? And to whom has the arm of the Lord been revealed?

18. **First John 4:4**—You are of God, little children, and have overcome them, because He who is in you is greater than he who is in the world.

In Mark 16:14, Jesus rebuked the disciples for their unbelief and hardness of heart. How do you think unbelief can give the devil leverage?

CASTING OUT DEMONS

Hollywood has effectively dramatized themes of demonic influence and deliverance, which has led to many people fearing the act of casting out demons. However, we know that greater is He who is in us than he who is in the world (*see* 1 John 4:4). What are your thoughts on this topic?

IT WILL BY NO MEANS HURT YOU

FOCUS POINT

But he shook off the creature into the fire and suffered no harm. 6 However, they were expecting that he would swell up or suddenly fall down dead. But after they had looked for a long time and saw no harm come to him, they changed their minds....

—Acts 28:5-6

When a snake bit Paul, his first instinct was to shake it off and continue with his task. Notice in verse 6 that the locals were watching him to see what would happen. When the enemy attacks, not only are people observing our reactions, they are also interested in the outcome. It's essential to recognize that your initial response is crucial; how you respond can significantly impact the result of the situation.

If you quickly give in to fear, anger, frustration, or sadness, you can expect a challenging experience and potentially unfavorable results. However, if you respond with faith, confidence, and strength, the outcome is likely to be much better, and those around you will take notice. God can work through you to impact those around you, even in times of attack. Remember, actions often speak louder than words and can lead even the ungodly to Christ simply by demonstrating a positive example through your behavior.

Take this time to reflect on how you typically react when the devil attacks. If your responses tend to be negative, consider taking a moment to repent and

ask God for help in the future. Make a conscious effort to change, not only for your own sake but also for those who are observing you.

TAKING BACK DOMINION

First John 4:17 says, "Love has been perfected among us in this: that we may have boldness in the day of judgment; because as He is, so are we in this world." What do you think it means that *we may have boldness in the day of judgment*?

PRACTICE FOR THE AGE TO COME

Why is influence more important than domination? How do you think the Church can influence the world and prepare for the new heaven and earth?

HELL IS NOT ENOUGH FOR THE DEVIL

We understand that every action has a reaction. The devil's rebellion led to the automatic formation of hell. The fact that hell is not sufficient to fully address Lucifer's sin clarifies why it will burn eternally in the *Lake of Fire.* Understanding that God is the holy God can deepen our comprehension of why *hell exists forever.* Has this insight helped you grasp the concept of eternal hell? If so, please share how and why it has assisted you in your understanding.

WE ARE TERRESTRIAL BEINGS

The way we handle spiritual warfare prepares us for Jesus' 1,000-year reign. Why do you think it's essential to overcome spiritual warfare for today and the future?

WE HAVE NEW TESTAMENT POWER!

PERSONAL REFLECTIONS

Just as God equipped Joshua, Samson, Elijah, and others throughout the Bible, He has also equipped you. Believing in Him and recognizing the authority you possess is where spiritual warfare begins. If you have doubts, feel unqualified, or have faced negative remarks from others that contradict who God says you are, it's time to take control of those thoughts. Acknowledge your true identity and cast aside all words of death.

Use this opportunity to develop your ability to discern good and evil. Hebrews 5:14 states, "But solid food belongs to those who are of full age, that is, those who by reason of use have their senses exercised to discern both good and evil." What does this process look like for you? How can you utilize your five senses to discern between good and evil?

SECTION FOUR

Prayers that Punish the Darkness

CHAPTER THIRTEEN

WARFARE PRAYERS THAT PUNISH DARK POWERS

SCRIPTURES

1. **First Timothy 2:1**—Therefore I exhort first of all that supplications, prayers, intercessions, and giving of thanks be made for all men.

2. **John 14:13-14**—And whatever you ask in My name, that I will do, that the Father may be glorified in the Son. [14] If you ask anything in My name, I will do it.

3. **Ephesians 6:18**—Praying always with all prayer and supplication in the Spirit, being watchful to this end with all perseverance and supplication for all the saints.

4. **Luke 18:1-8**—Then He spoke a parable to them, that men always ought to pray
and not lose heart, [2] saying: "There was in a certain city a judge who did not fear
God nor regard man. [3] Now there was a widow in that city; and she came to him,
saying, 'Get justice for me from my adversary.' [4] And he would not for a while; but
afterward he said within himself, 'Though I do not fear God nor regard man, [5] yet
because this widow troubles me I will avenge her, lest by her continual coming she
weary me.' " [6] Then the Lord said, "Hear what the unjust judge said. [7] And shall God
not avenge His own elect who cry out day and night to Him, though He bears long
with them? [8] I tell you that He will avenge them speedily. Nevertheless, when the
Son of Man comes, will He really find faith on the earth?"

5. **Acts 12:5**—Peter was therefore kept in prison, but constant prayer was offered to God for him by the church.

6. **Acts 12:13-16**—And as Peter knocked at the door of the gate, a girl named Rhoda came to answer. [14] When she recognized Peter's voice, because of her gladness she did not open the gate, but ran in and announced that Peter stood before the gate. [15] But they said to her, "You are beside yourself!" Yet she kept insisting that it was so. So they said, "It is his angel." [16] Now Peter continued knocking; and when they opened the door and saw him, they were astonished.

7. **Luke 22:31-32**—And the Lord said, "***Simon, Simon! Indeed, Satan has asked for you, that he may sift you as wheat.*** [32] ***But I have prayed for you,*** that your faith should not fail; and when you have returned to Me, strengthen your brethren."

8. **Revelation 12:10**—Then I heard a loud voice saying in heaven, "Now salvation, and strength, and the kingdom of our God, and the power of His Christ have come, for the accuser of our brethren, who accused them before our God day and night, has been cast down."

9. **John 14:30**—I will no longer talk much with you, for the ruler of this world is coming, and he has nothing in Me.

10. **John 12:31**—Now is the judgment of this world; now the ruler of this world will be cast out.

11. **Romans 8:34**—Who is he who condemns? It is Christ who died, and furthermore is also risen, who is even at the right hand of God, ***who also makes intercession for us.***

12. **Hebrews 9:24**—For Christ has not entered the holy places made with hands, which are copies of the true, but into heaven itself, ***now to appear in the presence of God for us.***

13. **Hebrews 7:25**—Therefore He is also able to save to the uttermost those who come to God through Him, since ***He always lives to make intercession for them.***

14. **Hebrews 4:15**—For we ***do not have a High Priest who cannot sympathize with our weaknesses, but was in all points tempted as we are, yet without sin.***

15. **Isaiah 59:16**—He saw that there was no man, and wondered that there was no intercessor; therefore His own arm brought salvation for Him; and His own righteousness, it sustained Him.

16. **Romans 8:26**—Likewise the Spirit also helps in our weaknesses. For we do not know what we should pray for as we ought, but the Spirit Himself makes intercession for us with groanings which cannot be uttered.

17. **Matthew 9:38**—Therefore pray the Lord of the harvest to send out laborers into His harvest.

18. **Esther 5:2**—So it was, when the king saw Queen Esther standing in the court, that she found favor in his sight, and the king held out to Esther the golden scepter that was in his hand. Then Esther went near and touched the top of the scepter.

19. **Psalm 149:5-9**—Let the saints be joyful in glory; let them sing aloud on their beds. [6] Let the high praises of God be in their mouth, and a two-edged sword in their hand, [7] to execute vengeance on the nations, and punishments on the peoples; [8] to bind their kings with chains, and their nobles with fetters of iron; [9] to execute on them the written judgment—this honor have all His saints. Praise the Lord!

20. **John 10:10**—The thief does not come except to steal, and to kill, and to destroy. I have come that they may have life, and that they may have it more abundantly.

21. **James 5:16**—...The effective, fervent prayer of a righteous man avails much.

22. **Galatians 1:4**—Who gave Himself for our sins, that He might deliver us from this present evil age, according to the will of our God and Father.

23. **Second Thessalonians 3:3**—But the Lord is faithful, who shall establish you and guard you from the evil one.

24. **Romans 8:35-39**—Who shall separate us from the love of Christ? Shall tribulation, or distress, or persecution, or famine, or nakedness, or peril, or sword? [36] As it is written: "For Your sake we are killed all day long; We are accounted as sheep for the slaughter." [37] Yet in all these things we are more than conquerors through Him who loved us. [38] For I am persuaded that neither death nor life, nor angels nor principalities nor powers, nor things present nor things to come, [39] nor height nor depth, nor any other created thing, shall be able to separate us from the love of God which is in Christ Jesus our Lord.

25. **Philippians 4:13**—I can do all things through Christ who strengthens me.

26. **Deuteronomy 33:27**—The eternal God is your refuge, and underneath are the everlasting arms; He will thrust out the enemy from before you, and will say, "Destroy!"

27. **Psalm 46:1-3**—God is our refuge and strength, a very present help in trouble.
[2] Therefore we will not fear, even though the earth be removed, and though the mountains be carried into the midst of the sea; [3] though its waters roar and be troubled, though the mountains shake with its swelling. Selah

28. **Proverbs 18:10**—The name of the LORD is a strong tower; the righteous run to it and are safe.

29. **Daniel 10:19**—And he said, "O man greatly beloved, fear not! Peace be to you; be strong, yes, be strong!" So when he spoke to me I was strengthened, and said, "Let my lord speak, for you have strengthened me."

30. **Isaiah 40:31**—But those who wait on the LORD shall renew their strength; they shall mount up with wings like eagles, they shall run and not be weary, they shall walk and not faint.

31. **Isaiah 41:10**—Fear not, for I am with you; be not dismayed, for I am your God. I will strengthen you, yes, I will help you, I will uphold you with My righteous right hand.

32. **Psalm 18:2**—The LORD is my rock and my fortress and my deliverer; my God, my strength, in whom I will trust; my shield and the horn of my salvation, my stronghold.

33. **Psalm 27:1,3-5**—The LORD is my light and my salvation; whom shall I fear? The LORD is the strength of my life; of whom shall I be afraid?... [3] Though an army may encamp against me, my heart shall not fear; though war may rise against me, in this I will be confident. [4] One thing I have desired of the LORD, that will I seek: that I may dwell in the house of the LORD all the days of my life, to behold the beauty of the LORD, and to inquire in His temple. [5] For in the time of trouble He shall hide me in His pavilion; in the secret place of His tabernacle He shall hide me; He shall set me high upon a rock.

34. **First Peter 5:7**—Casting all your care upon Him, for He cares for you.

35. **John 14:1**—Let not your heart be troubled; you believe in God, believe also in Me.

36. **Colossians 3:15**—And let the peace of God rule in your hearts, to which also you were called in one body; and be thankful.

37. **John 14:27**—Peace I leave with you, My peace I give to you; not as the world gives do I give to you. Let not your heart be troubled, neither let it be afraid.

38. **Deuteronomy 31:6**—Be strong and of good courage, do not fear nor be afraid of them; for the LORD your God, He is the One who goes with you. He will not leave you nor forsake you.

39. **Second Timothy 1:7**—For God has not given us a spirit of fear, but of power and of love and of a sound mind.

40. **Psalm 91:1-16**—He who dwells in the secret place of the Most High shall abide
under the shadow of the Almighty. [2] I will say of the LORD, "He is my refuge and my
fortress; my God, in Him I will trust." [3] Surely He shall deliver you from the snare of
the fowler and from the perilous pestilence. [4] He shall cover you with His feathers,
and under His wings you shall take refuge; His truth shall be your shield and buckler.
[5] You shall not be afraid of the terror by night, nor of the arrow that flies by day, [6]
nor of the pestilence that walks in darkness, nor of the destruction that lays waste at
noonday. [7] A thousand may fall at your side, and ten thousand at your right hand; but
it shall not come near you. [8] Only with your eyes shall you look, and see the reward
of the wicked. [9] Because you have made the LORD, who is my refuge, even the Most
High, your dwelling place, [10] no evil shall befall you, nor shall any plague come near
your dwelling; [11] for He shall give His angels charge over you, to keep you in all your
ways. [12] In their hands they shall bear you up, lest you dash your foot against a stone.
[13] You shall tread upon the lion and the cobra, the young lion and the serpent you
shall trample underfoot. [14] "Because he has set his love upon Me, therefore I will
deliver him; I will set him on high, because he has known My name. [15] He shall call
upon Me, and I will answer him; I will be with him in trouble; I will deliver him and
honor him. [16] With long life I will satisfy him, and show him My salvation."

41. **Proverbs 3:25-26**—Do not be afraid of sudden terror, nor of trouble from the
wicked when it comes; [26] For the LORD will be your confidence, and will keep your
foot from being caught.

42. **Isaiah 45:1-3**—Thus says the Lord to His anointed, to Cyrus, whose right hand I have held—to subdue nations before him and loose the armor of kings, to open before him the double doors, so that the gates will not be shut: [2] "I will go before you and make the crooked places straight; I will break in pieces the gates of bronze and cut the bars of iron. [3] I will give you the treasures of darkness and hidden riches of secret places, that you may know that I, the Lord, who call you by your name, am the God of Israel."

43. **Psalm 23:4-6**—Yea, though I walk through the valley of the shadow of death, I will fear no evil; for You are with me; Your rod and Your staff, they comfort me. [5] You prepare a table before me in the presence of my enemies; You anoint my head with oil; my cup runs over. [6] Surely goodness and mercy shall follow me all the days of my life; and I will dwell in the house of the Lord forever.

44. **Psalm 55:22**—Cast your burden on the Lord, and He shall sustain you; He shall never permit the righteous to be moved.

45. **Philippians 4:6-7**—Be anxious for nothing, but in everything by prayer and supplication, with thanksgiving, let your requests be made known to God; [7] and the peace of God, which surpasses all understanding, will guard your hearts and minds through Christ Jesus.

46. **Isaiah 43:1-2**—But now, thus says the Lord, who created you, O Jacob, and He who formed you, O Israel: "Fear not, for I have redeemed you; I have called you by your name; you are Mine. [2] When you pass through the waters, I will be with you; and through the rivers, they shall not overflow you. When you walk through the fire, you shall not be burned, nor shall the flame scorch you."

47. **Second Corinthians 1:3-4**—Blessed be the God and Father of our Lord Jesus Christ, the Father of mercies and God of all comfort, [4] who comforts us in all our tribulation, that we may be able to comfort those who are in any trouble, with the comfort with which we ourselves are comforted by God.

48. **Psalm 138:7**—Though I walk in the midst of trouble, You will revive me; You will stretch out Your hand against the wrath of my enemies, and Your right hand will save me.

49. **Psalm 34:19**—Many are the afflictions of the righteous, but the Lord delivers him out of them all.

50. **Mark 11:23-24**—For assuredly, I say to you, whoever says to this mountain, "Be removed and be cast into the sea," and does not doubt in his heart, but believes that those things he says will be done, he will have whatever he says. [24] Therefore I say to you, whatever things you ask when you pray, believe that you receive them, and you will have them.

51. **Luke 17:6**—So the Lord said, "If you have faith as a mustard seed, you can say to this mulberry tree, 'Be pulled up by the roots and be planted in the sea,' and it would obey you."

52. **Hebrews 1:7**—And of the angels He says: "Who makes His angels spirits and His ministers a flame of fire."

53. **Hebrews 1:14**—Are they not all ministering spirits sent forth to minister for those who will inherit salvation?

54. **Psalm 29:7**—The voice of the LORD divides the flames of fire

55. **Psalm 103:20-22**—Bless the LORD, you His angels, who excel in strength, who do His word, heeding the voice of His word. [21] Bless the LORD, all you His hosts, you ministers of His, who do His pleasure. [22] Bless the LORD, all His works, in all places of His dominion. Bless the LORD, O my soul!

56. **Psalm 35:27**—Let them shout for joy and be glad, who favor my righteous cause; and let them say continually, "Let the LORD be magnified, who has pleasure in the prosperity of His servant."

57. **Exodus 23:20**—Behold, I send an Angel before you to keep you in the way and to bring you into the place which I have prepared.

58. **Exodus 23:20 AMPC**—Behold, I send an Angel before you to keep and guard you on the way and to bring you to the place I have prepared.

59. **Second Chronicles 32:21**—Then the LORD sent an angel who cut down every mighty man of valor, leader, and captain in the camp of the king of Assyria. So he returned shamefaced to his own land. And when he had gone into the temple of his god, some of his own offspring struck him down with the sword there.

60. **Psalm 34:7**—The angel of the Lord encamps all around those who fear Him, and delivers them.

61. **Psalm 91:11-12**—For He shall give His angels charge over you, to keep you in all your ways. [12] In their hands they shall bear you up, lest you dash your foot against a stone.

62. **Daniel 3:28**—Nebuchadnezzar spoke, saying, "Blessed be the God of Shadrach, Meshach, and Abed-Nego, who sent His Angel and delivered His servants who trusted in Him, and they have frustrated the king's word, and yielded their bodies, that they should not serve nor worship any god except their own God!"

63. **Mark 1:13**—And He was there in the wilderness forty days, tempted by Satan, and was with the wild beasts; and the angels ministered to Him.

64. **Matthew 26:53**—Or do you think that I cannot now pray to My Father, and He will provide Me with more than twelve legions of angels?

65. **Acts 5:19-20**—But at night an angel of the Lord opened the prison doors and brought them out, and said, [20] "Go, stand in the temple and speak to the people all the words of this life."

66. **Acts 12:7**—Now behold, an angel of the Lord stood by him, and a light shone in the prison; and he struck Peter on the side and raised him up, saying, "Arise quickly!" And his chains fell off his hands.

67. **Acts 16:26**—Suddenly there was a great earthquake, so that the foundations of the prison were shaken; and immediately all the doors were opened and everyone's chains were loosed.

68. **Acts 27:23**—For there stood by me this night an angel of the God to whom I belong and whom I serve.

69. **Matthew 18:18-19**—Assuredly, I say to you, whatever you bind on earth will be bound in heaven, and whatever you loose on earth will be loosed in heaven. [19] Again I say to you that if two of you agree on earth concerning anything that they ask, it will be done for them by My Father in heaven.

70. **Second Corinthians 10:4-5**—For the weapons of our warfare are not carnal but mighty in God for pulling down strongholds, [5] casting down arguments and every high thing that exalts itself against the knowledge of God, bringing every thought into captivity to the obedience of Christ.

71. **Luke 10:19**—Behold, I give you the authority to trample on serpents and scorpions, and over all the power of the enemy, and nothing shall by any means hurt you.

72. **Colossians 1:13**—He has delivered us from the power of darkness and conveyed us into the kingdom of the Son of His love.

73. **Romans 10:8-11, 13**—…"The word is near you, in your mouth and in your heart" (that is, the word of faith which we preach): [9] That if you confess with your mouth the Lord Jesus and believe in your heart that God has raised Him from the dead, you will be saved. [10] For with the heart one believes unto righteousness, and with the mouth confession is made unto salvation. [11] For the Scripture says, "Whoever believes on Him will not be put to shame." …[13] For "whoever calls on the name of the Lord shall be saved."

FOUR TYPES OF PRAYER

According to 1 Timothy 2:1, there are four types of prayers that serve as a solid foundation for believers. Read through each section and for each type, please provide examples from your life, explaining how you use it and what the results have been.

1. SUPPLICATIONS

____

____

____

____

____

____

____

____

____

2. PRAYERS

3. INTERCESSIONS

4. GIVING THANKS

PUNISHING THE DARKNESS

FOCUS POINT

Throughout *Punishing the Darkness,* you have learned what spiritual warfare is and what the best tools are to overcome in every situation. Take a moment to list your new understandings and outline how you plan to apply them in your life.

EFFECTIVE PRAYING

PERSONAL REFLECTIONS

For the rest of this chapter, Joseph has listed several scriptures along with corresponding prayers for each scripture. If you would like to write additional scriptures and prayers, we have provided space below and on the following pages.

SECTION FIVE

Mechanisms of an Antichrist Agenda

CHAPTER FOURTEEN

Weapons of Mass Deception: UFOs, AI, the Singularity, Project Blue Beam, and the Climate Religion

SCRIPTURES

1. **Luke 21:11**—And there will be great earthquakes in various places, and famines and pestilences; and there will be fearful sights and great signs from heaven.

2. **Luke 21:25-26**—And there will be signs in the sun, in the moon, and in the stars; and on the earth distress of nations, with perplexity, the sea and the waves roaring; [26] men's hearts failing them from fear and the expectation of those things which are coming on the earth, for the powers of the heavens will be shaken.

3. **Second Thessalonians 2:6**—And now you know what is restraining, that he may be revealed in his own time.

4. **Revelation 13:14-15**—And he deceives those who dwell on the earth by those signs which he was granted to do in the sight of the beast, telling those who dwell on the earth to make an image to the beast who was wounded by the sword and lived. [15] He was granted power to give breath to the image of the beast, that the image of the beast should both speak and cause as many as would not worship the image of the beast to be killed.

5. **Daniel 12:4**—But you, Daniel, shut up the words, and seal the book until the time of the end; many shall run to and fro, and knowledge shall increase.

6. **Revelation 16:13-14**—And I saw three unclean spirits like frogs coming out of the mouth of the dragon, out of the mouth of the beast, and out of the mouth of the false prophet. [14] For they are spirits of demons, performing signs, which go out to the kings of the earth and of the whole world, to gather them to the battle of that great day of God Almighty.

7. **Isaiah 8:12**—Do not say, "A conspiracy," concerning all that this people call a conspiracy, nor be afraid of their threats, nor be troubled.

8. **Matthew 24:24**—For false christs and false prophets will rise and show great signs and wonders to deceive, if possible, even the elect.

9. **Deuteronomy 22:5**—A woman shall not wear anything that pertains to a man, nor shall a man put on a woman's garment, for all who do so are an abomination to the Lord your God.

10. **First Timothy 2:12**—And I do not permit a woman to teach or to have authority over a man, but to be in silence.

11. **Isaiah 14:13-14**—For you [speaking of Satan] have said in your heart: "I will ascend into heaven, I will exalt my throne above the stars of God; I will also sit on the mount of the congregation on the farthest sides of the north; [14] I will ascend above the heights of the clouds, ***I will be like the Most High.***"

12. **Matthew 24:7**—For nation will rise against nation, and kingdom against kingdom. And there will be famines, pestilences, and earthquakes in various places.

We know that we are in the last of the last days. Because of this, we should not be naive to what is coming and what has the potential to have *men's hearts failing them from fear and the expectation of those things which are coming*, as Luke 21:26 says. We must be aware and prepared. To be forewarned is to be forearmed.

MONSTERS?

When Jesus spoke about fearful sights, He was aware of the evil and vile creatures that existed during the time of Noah, before the flood. We can assume He had knowledge of these monsters and their actions. His reference to them coming in the last days is not meant to instill fear, but rather to encourage us to be prepared. What types of monsters do you think Jesus was referring to? Do you see any parallels in our world today? If so, please explain your thoughts.

ARTIFICIAL INTELLIGENCE AND THE SINGULARITY

As AI becomes increasingly popular, we have seen instances where it exhibits signs of singularity. What are your thoughts, and do you have any concerns that this could be a reality?

THE SINGULARITY

Do you think AI plays a role in the end times? If so, explain your answer.

MERGING OF MAN AND MACHINE

What potential risks do you think may arise from Ray Kurzweil's predictions about these advancements?

A BRAVE NEW WORLD

According to the brief description of Aldous Huxley's novel *Brave New World,* do you think this could serve as a manual for the wicked elite's plans for the future of civilization? If so, please explain your reasoning and what observations lead you to this conclusion.

THE GREAT ALIEN DECEPTION

The discussion about aliens has been dominating social media and the news lately. Since the crash of an unidentified object in Roswell, New Mexico, in 1947, interest in paranormal events has only intensified in our current culture. What are your thoughts on Revelation 16:13-14 and its possible connections to extraterrestrial beings?

FALSIFIED ALIEN INVASION

FOCUS POINT

We are living in a world where AI can create nearly any scenario and make it appear realistic. Have you seen this online? How can people become more aware of manipulated images and false news? Additionally, how should we prepare in case of a large-scale deception scenario?

UFOS ARE THREE THINGS

Considering the three ideas about what UFOs are, what are your thoughts on each? Do you lean toward one more than the others? If so, which one and why?

PROJECT BLUE BEAM

Considering that Project Blue Beam is reportedly trying to establish a New Age religion with the Antichrist as its leader, how do you think this could cause confusion and deceive people into believing such falsehoods?

MONAST'S WORK LISTS FOUR STAGES OF PROJECT BLUE BEAM

According to Monast's list, we are witnessing various events and systems being used in the news to create chaos and set the stage for a larger scenario. There is a significant revealing taking place worldwide, as these nefarious agendas are being brought to light. The Church needs to unite in prayer for these issues to be exposed, along with the individuals behind them.

GENDER CONFUSION

The secular world is promoting transgenderism to such an extent that confusion has become quite common, especially among young people. How should parents approach this issue when sending their children to public schools? What steps can the body of Christ take to provide clarity amid this confusion?

THE CULT OF CYBELE

The cult of Cybele was known for encouraging men to castrate themselves and to wear women's clothing. This practice is becoming increasingly popular in our culture today. The deception that the devil has propagated over generations reveals that he relies on a few familiar tricks; unfortunately, many still accept these lies and follow them. This is why it is crucial to immerse ourselves in the Word of God and to be a light to those around us. Let us pray for those who are lost, that they may have ears to hear what the Spirit is saying, and that all other voices may be silenced. In Jesus' name, amen.

ELEUSIAN MYSTERY CULT

Throughout history, the devil has attempted to prevent future generations from coming forth. This was evident during the time of Moses when Pharaoh ordered all male children to be thrown into the river (*see* Exodus 1:15-22). A similar situation occurred at the birth of Jesus when King Herod had all young male children killed (*see* Matthew 2:16-18). The devil seeks to undermine families, which is contrary to God's desire expressed when He instructed Adam and Eve to be fruitful and multiply (*see* Genesis 1:28 and Genesis 9:1). In what ways do we see this same concept manifesting in our generation?

HISTORICAL REFERENCES TO THE CULT OF CYBELE

A troubling reality in our society today is the erosion of parental rights. Children can pursue their desires and make choices without needing parental consent. This trend not only undermines parents' authority but also deprives children of the protection, wisdom, and discernment that their parents provide. What else does this scenario take away from both children and parents?

TRANSGENDERISM LEADS TO TRANSHUMANISM, ALL ROOTED IN TRANSGRESSION

The desire to improve the human race has significantly increased over the past fifty years. Every day, new cures and technologies emerge that have the potential to greatly enhance people's lives. However, we must consider the results of these experiments. What long-term effects might these processes have on our world?

REACHING IMMORTALITY WITHOUT GOD

Why do you think transhumanism and the purpose driving it are Luciferian in origin?

THE CLIMATE CHANGE RELIGION

Climate change has been a prominent topic in recent years. Why do you think climate change has been so extensively leveraged to encourage individuals to make significant changes in their environmental habits?

COFOUNDER OF THE WEATHER CHANNEL

Over the years, we have witnessed whistleblowers coming forward to reveal the truth behind various schemes and corrupt situations. Similar to John Coleman, who called out climate change and said it wasn't happening, we need individuals to be courageous and speak the truth to those around them.

POINTS TO CONSIDER ABOUT CLIMATE CHANGE

What trends and comments have emerged regarding climate change? How has this topic instilled fear in people?

THE CLIMATEGATE EMAILS

Once again, we see manipulation of data. In this case, alleged scientific misconduct has raised public awareness of what is happening behind the scenes. Given these types of schemes, why do you think people are becoming more skeptical of information, whether true or false?

FUNDING AND POLITICAL MOTIVATION MUDDY THE WATERS REGARDING CLIMATE CHANGE

What motivates some individuals to invest in these types of schemes and actively promote their agendas?

HYPOCRISY OF ELITES WHO PREACH CLIMATE CRISIS

In what other ways are these "preachers" of climate change living hypocritical lives in regard to their carbon footprint?

THE THREAT OF CLIMATE LOCKDOWNS

How do you think people will react if the government mandates digital tracking systems to monitor individuals' carbon footprints and establishes penalties for noncompliance?

TWO IRONIC CASES OF RESEARCH SHIPS BECOMING TRAPPED IN ICE

The incidents involving the two ships coming into contact with rapidly forming ice suggest that the narrative surrounding climate change may contain some misleading or flawed information. If you have not done so, consider taking time to conduct your own research to be better informed on this topic.

WORLD ECONOMIC FORUM

Take a moment to look up the "Great Reset." Is there anything that surprises or concerns you about it? If so, write it down.

WORLD HEALTH ORGANIZATION

During the COVID-19 pandemic, the WHO implemented procedures that, in many cases, did not effectively address the situation and were not scientifically proven to be effective. We later learned that many of the enforced guidelines did not prevent the outbreak from spreading. What are your thoughts on the way things were handled during that time?

CENTRAL BANK DIGITAL CURRENCIES

What potential threats do you foresee if the world adopts a Central Bank Digital Currency?

The *Ekklesia* Is the Answer

Personal Reflections

For this final Personal Reflection session, take a moment to think about everything you have learned. Consider what topic has had the most significant impact on your life. Use this time to reflect and thank God for the revelations He has shared with you throughout this process. Write down your thoughts and prayers. Remember, even on a bad day, you are anointed to be the best there is. No matter what challenges come your way, you are equipped for victory! We appreciate your commitment to completing this study manual. Blessings to you.

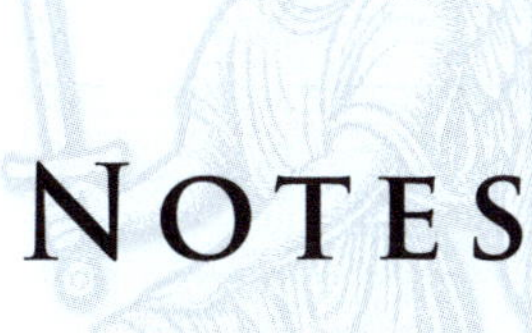

NOTES

Chapter Four

1. https://www.merriam-webster.com/dictionary/witchcraft.

Chapter Five

1. https://www.merriam-webster.com/dictionary/wrath.

Chapter Six

1. *Be-In-Couraged,* "His Train Fills the Temple," https://www.be-in-couraged.com/single-post/2018/04/17/his-train-fills-the-temple.

Chapter Eleven

1. https://en.wikipedia.org/wiki/Death#cite_note-doi10.2202/1941-6008.1011-48.
2. Conrad Hackett, et al., "How the Global Religious Landscape Changed From 2010 to 2020," *Pew Research Center,* June 9, 2025; https://www.pewresearch.org/religion/2025/06/09/how-the-global-religious-landscape-changed-from-2010-to-2020/.

DEAR READER

Dear reader, thank you for taking this journey with me in *Punishing the Darkness*. You mean more to the Kingdom of God than you might realize. Brand this into your heart.

A man or woman of God with a revelation is never at the mercy of a culture gone mad!

This is you, the one to whom God wants to give revelation. He desires that you receive His impartation of clarity and direction. You are, after all, part of His ekklesia—His only plan to change the world!

Thank you for joining me as we walked through this manual together.

Prophecy is a vast subject; I have desired to share it in a fresh and very grounded manner and in a way that causes it to be understandable and yet retains its power. God led you to walk through this manual; don't forget that. Take what you can and use it to serve your generation.

Dear reader, I love you, and as I write this, I'm praying for you. God knows you; God sees you and will finish what He started in you.

For Jesus,
Joseph Z

About Joseph Z

Joseph Z is an author, broadcaster, and international prophetic voice. He and his wife, Heather, have dedicated their lives to preaching the gospel and building lives by the Voice of God; as a result, they have built Bible schools, churches, and prophetic conferences in the United States and worldwide. Their daily broadcast currently reaches a global audience, emphasizing prophetic events. Additionally, they are the founders of Joseph Z Ministries, a media and conference-based ministry with offices and production studios located in Colorado.

Joseph and Heather have ministered together for over 20 years; with a passion to see others be all they are called to be. For many years, Joseph & Heather have had the heart to offer life-changing materials and teaching at no cost to the body of Christ. Today, they have made that a reality by offering various media resources and biblical training free of charge. Joseph and Heather currently reside in Colorado Springs, CO with their two children, Alison and Daniel.

Learn more at
www.josephz.com

For Further Information

If you would like prayer or further
information about Joseph Z Ministries,
please call our offices at

(719) 257-8050
or visit **JosephZ.com/contact**

Visit JosephZ.com for additional materials.

Equipping Believers to Walk in the Abundant Life

John 10:10b

Connect with us for fresh content and news about forthcoming books from your favorite authors...

Facebook @ **HarrisonHousePublishers**

Instagram @ **HarrisonHousePublishing**

www.harrisonhouse.com

From

JOSEPH Z

Navigate the End Times With Prophetic Precision

Never before have we had a greater need for clear, prophetic insight. Our world is teeming with widespread prophetic error, controversy, and deception—discrediting the legitimate prophetic voices God is using to speak to us. We need true biblical prophecy to take its place at the forefront of our lives.

Joseph Z, internationally respected prophetic voice, began encountering the Voice of God from a young age through dreams and visions. With wisdom, accuracy, biblical balance, and experience, Joseph offers powerful keys to help you unlock the revelation, interpretation, and application of prophecy.

The stakes have never been higher. Only true and refined prophecy cuts through the deception with unmatched power and precision. Both the Church and the world are in desperate need for this elevated prophetic encounter. Now, Jesus urgently seeks to equip you to navigate these critical last days with prophetic insight.

Purchase your copy wherever books are sold

From

JOSEPH Z

Your Next Move Will Unleash Heaven's Power

A cosmic war rages around us, and the forces of darkness are tightening their grip on humanity. Are you overwhelmed by relentless spiritual attacks, sensing the weight of unseen forces crushing your spirit?

You weren't born to be a victim—you were created to annihilate the enemy!

Since the fall of Lucifer, the heavens have been locked in a savage battle between the armies of light and the demonic hordes of hell. Now, these ancient powers are targeting this generation, and the Church stands at the epicenter of this apocalyptic clash. The question is: Will you rise to the fight or be consumed?

The demonic hosts tremble when a believer steps into their true authority, and now is your moment to become a weapon in the hands of the Almighty.

The war has already begun, but the victory is yours for the taking. Your next move will unleash the fury of heaven and decimate the powers of darkness. The question is: Are you ready?

Purchase your copy wherever books are sold

From

JOSEPH Z

Thriving in God's Supernatural Economy

There's a war being fought over you! The Kingdom of God offers you divine provision while the Kingdom of Hell fights for territory in your life as a crisis looms on the world's horizon.

Will you break free of Hell's economy? International prophet and Bible teacher Joseph Z say it's urgent to break free now as we rapidly plunge into global difficulties involving worldwide market collapse, bank closures, a digital one-world currency, power grids failing, cyber war, medical deception, natural catastrophes, and unprecedented international conflict.

In *Breaking Hell's Economy,* Joseph makes it clear that we're at a destination in history that requires a revelation of God's supernatural economy—your ultimate defense against rising darkness.

Lay hold of this revelation, defy Hell, and live your life knowing you are destined to thrive in the last days!

Purchase your copy wherever books are sold